Failing School, Failing City

Failing School, Failing City

The reality of inner city education

Martin Johnson

Jon Carpenter

Our books may be ordered from bookshops or (post free) from
Jon Carpenter Publishing, 2 The Spendlove Centre, Charlbury,
England OX7 3PQ

Please send for our free catalogue

Credit card orders should be phoned or faxed to 01689 870437
or 01608 811969

Our US distributor is Paul and Company, PO Box 442, Concord, MA 01742
(phone 978 369 3049, fax 978 369 2385)

First published in 1999 by
Jon Carpenter Publishing
2 The Spendlove Centre, Charlbury, Oxfordshire OX7 3PQ
☎ 01608 811969

ISBN 1 897766 41 6

Printed in England by J. W. Arrowsmith Ltd., Bristol.
Cover printed by KMS Litho, Hook Norton

Contents

INTRODUCTION

N O BRITISH CITIZEN, surely, can be in any doubt that education is the current passion of politicians of all parties, and particularly of the Labour government. Like the rest of us, the politicians are able to feed their passion by reading a gushing stream of books explaining how it is, how it could be, and how it should be. Somehow, though, teachers hear the hot-blooded words with sinking hearts, because many of those words just do not ring true.

Little of what is written and spoken by pundits and politicians seems to grasp what it's really like to teach in English schools today, particularly those serving working class communities in our cities. All my friends and colleagues who teach in such classrooms feel the same.

Like many of my colleagues, I have waited for the real story to be told. But I see no sign. So I have written this book. It is a teacher's story. It tells it how it is in inner city secondary education.

Why me, why now? In early 1997, I was invited to contribute a small piece to a radio programme describing what it's like to be a teacher in a city school. The studio pundits were polite but clearly despised my apparent pessimism and desperation. One reviewer, however, thought she heard an authentic voice. Colleagues also found it unexceptional. I was simply voicing ordinary staff-room talk. It was then I decided that this growing gap between practitioners and pundits had to be advertised.

What are my credentials? I started teaching in 1969, at a huge and dynamic comprehensive school on the outskirts of Liverpool, which served exclusively the disadvantaged and the dispossessed. After a brief stay in West Yorkshire, I returned to my birthplace, London, where I have lived and taught ever since. I have specialised in working with pupils with behaviour difficulties, both in mainstream classes, and in units both attached to and detached from schools. For a number of years, I have also had the opportunity to visit many schools, and listen to many teachers talk about their working lives.

This book is an attempt to explain to decision makers, opinion formers, and others, what really goes on in classrooms in inner city schools. I hope it may also suggest some ways of improving the situation, which currently is dire. No doubt my interpretations will be dismissed by many, including thrusting school improver headteachers, and plenty of others responsible for the condition of schooling in the country, as well as professors with bright ideas.

Of course, headteachers will be forced to deny that anything like what I describe is a realistic picture of their schools. These are the same headteachers who feel obliged not to return official forms reporting assaults and other threats to their schools' health and safety. In the current competitive market climate, how can headteachers admit publicly to any shortcomings in their schools? Since local authorities in the present system find it very difficult to know what is happening in their schools, and since the headteachers are their correspondents, how can local government know or speak the truth?

I prefer to be judged by my peers. If the generality of classroom teachers in the city claim that what follows is nonsense, then it will have no value. But if, on the other hand, they claim that I do indeed tell it how it is, then the complaints of the others will not hurt.

It is necessary to be clear about my argument, and about the focus of this book. I am a secondary teacher, and I have no direct experience of primary schools, although I visit primary schools and listen to primary colleagues. Obviously, as children grow up, their behaviour and attitudes develop. My observations are of secondary schools, and my argument applies strictly to secondary schools. However, no-one would assume that the situation I describe only appears as children move to the big school, and primary teachers have their own versions of the same realities. Indeed, I make specific reference in places to the primary situation.

One difference, however, is interesting, and cause for optimism in the long term. Primary teachers report that parents and carers of all classes virtually universally hope that their tots will learn to read and write, and thus in some sense have a positive attitude to education. Amongst the underclass, however, the attitude may be expressed belligerently, and the belligerence may increase as the child becomes a literacy failure during the primary phase. By the time of secondary transfer, the failure may provoke a renewed rejection of education.

I am writing about schools in England. It seems that similar problems connected with educating the underclass are found in other advanced western societies, but I do not write about the overspill slums of Paris, nor of the way it is in Cardiff, Glasgow, or Belfast. I expect there to be some commonality of experience, but with different details.

Re-introducing social class

I am writing about pupils from a particular social class, which I call the underclass. In the eyes of many, this immediately consigns me to the ark. 'Look, we did all that in the sixties. We've moved on now. It's schools that make the difference.'

My belief is that progress in defeating underachievement is inhibited when the importance of class as a determinant of educational success is ignored, or even denied. It is a long time since research showed this link, and since then the focus has moved on to other contributory factors, principally the effectiveness of the individual school. Indeed, class is now hardly a respectable concept anywhere within political discourse. Yet the relationship has never been challenged, much less disproved; it has been simply forgotten.

Since sociologists made the connection over thirty years ago, there have been substantial changes in social and cultural structures. I argue that the now permanent situation of mass unemployment has created a new class, an underclass. Its members are separated from the rest of society by what appears to them to be a permanent inability to sustain themselves economically. The separation creates its own class identity and class culture, which is antagonistic to the rest of society, and to the state. State education is one of the institutions which bears the brunt of this antagonism.

I do not think this analysis is contentious, although others might wish to use other language. Unfortunately, these others, including education policy makers, seem to wish to avoid mentioning it. It is often said that talking in these terms is negative, excuses educational failure, and condones low expectations amongst teachers. What teachers must do, runs the argument, is be determined to eradicate failure by concentrating on things they can change, rather than factors they cannot. School improvement will solve the problem.

I argue the opposite. The single-minded emphasis on school improvement will fail, precisely because it ignores the key determinants of achievement. I do not condone low expectations of underclass pupils. The anger in this book is evidence enough of the frustration I feel at the waste of talent, at the damaged lives, at the pain and misery of my pupils and their families. I know that thousands of my colleagues share my feelings. Yet my experience teaches me that we cannot improve things unless we start from a realistic analysis of the situation, and that must include a recognition of social class factors in educational success.

The school for the underclass

I am writing, then, about a small minority of secondary schools in England. Schools all over the country have some pupils from families who are negative about education. Whether serving cities, large or small towns, or a mainly rural population, the majority of English schools have a degree of social mixture in their intakes, including some who, for personal or cultural reasons, do not share the schools' aims and values. These pupils and their families are a challenge for all teachers, a challenge they accept.

I am not writing about those schools or those pupils. I am writing about what I shall call, for the sake of brevity, *schools for the underclass*. Needless to say, they are to be found in or adjacent to areas populated by the underclass, that is to say, in the inner city and the estates and the communities dying from the loss of their industries.

In other words, such schools are found all over the country, because poverty and unemployment are found all over the country. London, of course, has greater extremes of wealth and poverty than anywhere else, but it by no means corners the market in underclass schools. However, they cannot be defined in terms of their geography; as I shall show, not all schools in the inner city are schools for the underclass, and schools close to each other geographically may be far apart socially.

No, *they are defined by their intake*. In the schools I describe in this book, a large proportion of the pupils are from the underclass. There are, perhaps, only a handful in the country where the intake is almost completely from the underclass. Nevertheless, just as grammar schools are middle class institutions in every way, even if they have a strong minority of working class pupils, so underclass schools are underclass institutions even if they have a strong minority of working class pupils. I am not able to state a defining percentage: if x% of the intake comes from the underclass, it is an underclass school. I am not sure whether such a figure exists, although one authority, Professor Peter Mortimore, has recently suggested 60%. Such schools need to be categorised by qualitative rather than quantitative means.

The culture of the underclass dominates these schools. These are the schools which are the focus of this book. In short, I am describing that minority of secondary schools in England whose intake consistently contains a proportion of children of underclass origins sufficient to become the strongest single determinant of the life of those schools.

Even in schools for the underclass, there will be a substantial proportion of pupils whose parents continue to have aspirations within mainstream society. They might be in work, they might be unemployed, but the significant difference between them and their underclass neighbours is that they still try to hope and believe that there can be a future for themselves, or at least for their offspring. They may not know the ropes, in the sense of knowing how to help their children up the educational selection greasy pole, but they believe in the power of education as the route to economic advance, and exhort their children to do their best.

These young people of the working class are in a position as difficult as that of the working class child in the grammar school in the old days, for they are within an institution with not one but two other cultures. On the one hand, the staff and the 'official' values, so middle class. On the other hand, the dominant group of pupils, the rejectionists. The underclass youths look as least as aggressive and threatening to classmates who are inclined to try to get some work done as they do to the staff who are trying to contain them.

It may well be an almost universal feature of English schools that the 'boffins', those who appear interested in school work, are generally derided if not bullied, but it is particularly powerful when at work in the school for the underclass. As I shall describe, the rejectionists do indeed dominate the classrooms. By definition, they are the ones creating the incidents, diverting the teacher, causing the noise, stopping the lessons. Working class pupils are stuck in the middle, not wishing to take sides in the conflict, and not able to side with teachers. Yet they become the focus of attention and hope for the teachers, for they still have potential, and just maybe they can be helped to remain in education and to become successful. Every teacher has to retain that hope.

In inner city schools, then, pupils will display varieties of attainment, of motivation, of attitudes to schooling. Some of the differences are due to personality, some to family, and some to wider culture. The focus of this book is on that minority of schools where the pupil mix is such that the dominant attitude is negative, the dominant level of achievement is low, and the classroom is a site of continuous struggle for the teacher to gain and retain control.

Three reasons for this focus

I have no way of knowing the number of such schools across the country, but most schools are not like that, and most schools in the city are not quite like that. Why should I give so much attention to such a small minority of schools? As a teacher, should I not be trumpeting the achievements of my colleagues in the large majority of schools? There are three answers.

First, these schools, though in a different form, have been given a high political and media profile. I discuss later the relationship between 'underclass school' and 'failing school' as defined by Ofsted. Suffice it to say that there is considerable correspondence. Dealing with failing schools and failing teachers has become a preoccupation of governments. The employment of slogans and quick-fix initiatives gives the impression of dynamism and progress. However, it is necessary to be rigorous in analysis and honest in policy if the realities are to be addressed, and I have not found much of either within the discourse on failing schools.

I believe it is necessary to begin to address the problem of the under-achievement of the many in our schools by describing honestly what goes on. Achievement will not be improved radically either by frequent measurement of achievement or by exhortation. I believe that special measures are neces-sary to address the issue in the schools for the underclass. I use the term special measures advisedly, but I do not have in mind the kind of measures imposed on failing schools by Ofsted.

The second reason for concentrating on underclass schools is that it is time someone told the truth about the sheer awfulness of working in them. Many teachers come, they see — and they make a hasty retreat, and I do not blame them. As far as I am concerned, the teachers that stick it out, many of them for years and years, are saints. Nobody should have to work day after day, year after year, in the conditions faced by teachers in such schools. Quite apart from the educational needs of the pupils, the staffs need action to relieve them of the impossible stress, which ruins the health of so many who work there.

Am I over-dramatic? I write what I have seen. Why is this not reported? It is not in anyone's interests to report these things. Ofsted does not have to record staff casualties; headteachers and local authorities wish to put the best gloss on their schools; the teachers themselves have no-one to complain to, and would face the sack for 'bringing the school into disrepute'. But telling the truth is just something that has to be done. The majority of the staffs of these schools are supported by a personal commitment to their pupils, an ambition to help them overcome their disadvantage, a vocation which is retained despite the very low success rates that result from their self-sacrificing efforts. It is time the nation heard the truth about these heroes, rewarded them, and stood them down.

The third reason is that although what I describe applies fully only to a few schools, there are reflections of the same phenomena across the large majority of our secondary schools which serve the working class. Of course, all social categorisations are arbitrary, and distort a infinitely complex reality. I use the categories underclass school, working class school, and so on, in an unprob-lematic way, but the distortion to reality would be reduced by placing all our secondary schools on a continuum with regard to characteristics such as degree of order, or ease of compliance. In other words, *the behaviour and attitudes which I describe are seen at their most extreme in the underclass school, but appear to a greater or lesser extent in a very large proportion of our secondary schools.* There are few schools in which indiscipline is not a major inhibitor of attainment.

Amongst all the meaningless statistics collected by Ofsted, there is one measurement which would be revealing but which is not taken. What proportion of teaching time do pupils spend 'on task', that is actually performing the activity which is planned for that lesson? Such a measurement would reveal the difficulties faced by all teachers in a wide range of schools in maintaining the concentration of their pupils on what they should be doing.

Teachers in all kinds of schools believe that it is becoming more problematic for the averagely competent teacher to gain and retain the attention and compliance of pupils. The problem is seen as worst in inner city schools, and likely to apply with decreasing force in ratio to the geographical and cultural distance from those schools.

That is not to say that the tendency approaches zero in what some continue to consider as England's rural idylls. Teachers there have to face rural poverty and the darker sides of village life. In addition, stories circulate amongst the teaching community of, say, Shropshire, about the trials and tribulations of their colleagues in the more difficult schools in Telford. We have to attack the problem of massive underachievement in the underclass school, but we have also to attack the general problem in our schools of underachievement caused by lack of order, lack of time on task, and lack of peer approval in being a learner.

Teachers and the breakdown of discipline

There might appear to be some congruence here with the views expressed by commentators who complain of the collapse of discipline in our schools. In some cases, the explanation for this appears to be the unwillingness or inability of teachers, armed by philosophies from the contract theorists onwards, to impose discipline.

I can assure urban myth generators that those who wish for a laisser-faire, let-a-hundred-flowers-blossom regime for their children in contemporary Britain must pay for it in those very few private schools still remaining which maintain the Summerhill tradition of granting autonomy to the children. No doubt there are many teachers, particularly in primary schools, who retain a sneaking regard for such ideas, but they would neither dare nor be permitted to implement them in their classrooms. The William Tyndale affair, over twenty years ago, eradicated the small pockets of that kind of permissive approach.

No, the instinct for self-preservation dictates that teachers wish for classes which will be compliant to their reasonable instructions. The total absence of that condition in the underclass school, and its partial absence in other schools, is a major negative factor in most teachers' working lives.

As for explaining current issues in schools in terms of the likes of Locke, Rousseau and Dewey, teachers simply do not have the luxury of contemplating competing philosophies of education, of revisiting their experiences to reconsider the great 'ought-to-be' questions. Neither is their practice based in their previous philosophical inquiry, now embedded as determining assumptions. Teachers teach what they are told, when they are told, how they are told. Teachers have little professional autonomy. The people who do the telling are under similar pressure. It's all about National Curriculum levels, SATs, GCSEs.

As a young teacher, I remember slumping in the staff-room on a Friday afternoon, and after a recovery period of desultory conversation, getting into heated debates about the point of it all, what our pupils really needed, how we could remake the world through education, or whether that was possible. Often as not, some of us would continue the debate in the pub. We were young, we were committed, and we thought we could make a difference.

I am sad to say I don't think this kind of thing happens very much now. In those days, if we thought some new syllabus, or even some new subject, was needed, we could introduce it, if our ideas passed inspection, and our pupils could get a CSE in it. These days, young teachers feel themselves as cogs in the machine, having no control over syllabus, assessment, or teaching method. What is there to discuss?

I believe that the real situation is almost the opposite of that proposed by these commentators. Older teachers, at least, remain more committed than the population as a whole to values of community, ethical behaviour, a certain disdain for conspicuous consumption, and to concepts of discipline and self-discipline. I fear that younger teachers, Thatcher's generation, are less opposed to the rampant individualism which now marks our social relations, but schools in general, far from being part of this trend, much less a major cause of it, are one of the few social institutions which continue to resist.

I believe that disorder in school and in society is much better explained in terms of the real conditions of existence we all experience, and in the ways of living and attitudes which these conditions produce. We need to look at the forces of consumerism in our society, and at the alienation within our underclass, for an understanding of the ways our children behave.

It is true that education professionals tend to treat these questions very much as psychological rather than sociological matters. That is understandable, since a child with behaviour problems has to be dealt with as an individual. Teachers would not take kindly to an educational psychologist's report on a pupil which concluded that he was suffering from alienation and the treatment was for his family to be placed on a permanently secure economic footing.

Teachers must work day by day with individual human beings, and tend to work with psychological categories. It is beyond their scope to intervene in the broader picture, but that does not mean they do not have some understanding of that picture and the way it impinges on them and their schools.

However, this book is about those schools at the extreme of the continuum. My thesis is that their condition is difficult enough to be qualitatively different from the vast majority of schools in the country. Yes, order is a problem in most schools, but it will be amenable to conventional solutions as soon as it is openly recognised. In the school for the underclass, however, quite unconventional innovation is necessary if order is to be restored.

The teachers, or the pupils?

There is another way in which this book is outside the mainstream of the current discourse on schools and achievement. It focuses on the pupils, not the teachers. It locates explanations for pupil failure amongst the pupils, not the teachers. All the evidence suggests that the overwhelming proportion of differences in attainment is due to pupil characteristics rather than school or teacher characteristics, however much politicians and others appear to believe otherwise.

I realise that this is a dangerous way of thinking. It is an *explanation* for underachievement, but of course it could become an *excuse* for it. The school improvement movement was based on the need to get away from deterministic attitudes, and to concentrate on those factors which can be influenced by the professionals. We all have to work on that basis, and all teachers have to believe that they can make a difference.

The damage has been caused by going too far the other way. To pretend, as is now commonplace, that we can ignore intake is to be dangerously unrealistic. Such a bald statement is never made in that way. However, much of the current discourse only makes sense if such an assumption underlies it. The mere existence of raw score performance tables carries that implication, however much their supporters talk about the need to insert value-added indicators as well. In particular, the treatment by Ofsted and the government of schools with an underclass intake is the clearest example of the futile policy directions which result from this assumption.

The whole focus within school improvement is on what teachers do. It is argued that improvement in results occurs when the teachers work harder, change their practices, raise their expectations of pupils, and so on. In the real world, however, the usual way to improve results is actually to import some pupils from more favoured backgrounds; the trick is how to achieve that. The truth is that the same teacher using the same methods achieves vastly different results in two different schools. We all know this, and it does not help when the whole of current educational policy seems to depend on its denial.

Not to bear in mind that differences in attainment are due mainly to pupil characteristics is to inhibit realistic policies. We need a balance here. We need to admit that while institutions can make a difference, that difference is minor, in comparison with the variations due to intake.

When we do that, we can start to look again at why pupils do not learn. We can get out that old research, and re-analyse it in today's context. We can think again about the cultures brought into school, we can look again at what pupils do in classrooms, we can go back to policies which intervene where it matters.

A recent report, *Literacy, Numeracy, and Economic Performance*, by Peter Robinson, made just this point: 'a serious programme to alleviate child poverty might do far more for boosting attainment ... than any modest intervention in schooling.' The report disappeared without trace. It is not yet respectable again to point out that Britain has greater economic and social inequality than any other European nation, and that there just might be a connection between that and comparisons of educational achievement.

The incompetent teachers

If that balance were restored, perhaps there would be an end to blaming teachers for the poor performance of some groups of pupils. No-one should underestimate the effects on the profession of the so-called teacher bashing of recent years. As well as attacking morale, it remains a major disincentive to recruitment. In reality, that crude public phase ended, more or less, some time ago, but its effect was so great that many, perhaps most, colleagues have not yet noticed. They continue, however, to receive the same message from all the agencies which proclaim that pupil achievement is not good enough.

I am disinclined to criticise the profession in any way when others have done the job so much more comprehensively than I could manage. Nevertheless, I do not wish to appear to believe that every single teacher in the country is equally and brilliantly competent. All teachers resent the truly incompetent colleague, because that person makes the job harder for everyone else in the school. Until very recently, however, employers virtually never had the skills or the determination to tackle those rare cases.

It would be a significant mistake, however, to see the quality of the workforce as a significant factor in lack of pupil achievement. As Ofsted

consistently reports, the very great majority of lessons are taught at least satisfactorily. In their school careers, pupils can expect to be taught adequately
nearly all of the time. On occasion, they will come across an outstandingly
talented teacher. If they are unlucky, at one stage they will meet an inadequate
teacher. In the nature of things, some teachers are better at their job than
others, but the experience of most pupils and their parents across most schools
is that the incompetent teacher is the exception, not the rule.

As I explain later, competence is an issue of much greater salience in the
underclass school. Firstly, ordinary teachers cannot survive there. They come,
they see, they leave. Only extraordinary teachers can stay, remain committed,
and continue to produce quality performance, and become part of that core
staff who are the essential stabilising influence on the school. Secondly, many
extraordinary teachers are not drawn to such schools, but look for greater
rewards at less personal cost. A major part of the story of the underclass
school is the permanent shortage of those staff who have what it takes in that
most difficult of environments.

Of course it is true that the generality of teachers, like those in every other
occupation, could improve their practice if offered appropriate training. I
believe the shortage of really useful in-service training is a major impediment
to improvement. A recent report by Cooper and Lybrand highlighted the poor
quality of human resource management in education; the constant exhortations to improve are seldom accompanied by the tools to achieve the
improvement.

The need for quality recruits, for quality initial and in-service training, for
procedures for monitoring performance, are all undeniable. These issues,
however, are not the major focus of this book because they are not the major
determinant of educational success. Educational success is produced by
pupils who are motivated and able.

It is unfortunate that government agencies have supported politicians in the
contrary assumption. The key assertion is that schools with similar intakes
have widely differing outcomes. I shall show that this assertion is entirely
false, and backed up by spurious statistical juggling.

My story

So this is a different kind of story about schools in the city and on the
estates. It sees life within them as determined more by the pupils than the
teachers. It sees new economic and social policies as more important for
achievement than education gimmicks. It sees schools continually on or over
the edge of disorder. It sees teachers there as a beleaguered set of heroes,
hanging on despite everything.

This is not the story anyone wants told. Everyone else in education has reasons for burying it. It is, however, the truth as I have experienced it, and as thousands of my colleagues suffer it.

The essence of the book is in the opening chapter, where I describe what happens, in reality, in some secondary classrooms. I describe only what I have observed. The schools I used for these observations are of one kind: their intake is overwhelmingly from the urban underclass, and they are failing, in the Ofsted sense. I then go on to consider the social backgrounds of the pupils from such schools, and to try to bring back into the discourse on school performance the old truth that output depends on intake. This gives rise to further discussion of some of the features of such schools and the job of teaching within them, within the context of current education policies. No book on this subject would be complete without a look at Ofsted's contribution to underclass achievement, from the teacher's perspective.

Readers who get that far, but no further, will no doubt dismiss me as just another whinger, as part of the problem not the solution, as your typically negative self-justifying wrecker. The insistence from day one that the 'new Labour' government would have no time for the whingers, and would only deal with those who were within the 'can-do' mind-set, is indeed a matter of concern. This ploy is being used to close off debate, to debunk all those who dare to disagree. After years in which decision-makers were regarded by most teachers as inhabiting some other planet, we had hoped for a resumption of realism.

It is not only right, but essential, to test proposals for improving our schools against what is known about their present condition. It is no good pretending that things are not as they are. A reforming government, as Labour governments profess to be, should be prepared to accept evidence presented to it by a range of authorities about the efficacy of its ideas. It is unhealthy for the DfEE to surround itself with a small body of the like-minded, and to exclude contrary views. The politicisation of the office of Her Majesty's Chief Inspector increases the difficulty of the government in obtaining dispassionate advice.

I do not see myself as negative, but as realistic. If the focus is on 'the long tail of underachievement', to quote recent jargon, then it must be right to look closely at the underachievers in school before trying to improve the situation. In the first part of this book, I simply try to describe the reality of education for the underachieving underclass. I hope, however, that the second part of the book will be seen as more positive. In it, I offer some suggestions for ways forward, and discuss some of the suggestions of the government and others. Some of them will be unpopular because they cost money, but I believe my ideas overall are not expensive because the alternatives cost more.

At the end, I come back to the beginning. The schools in any society are a reflection of that society. As the eminent academic Basil Bernstein showed many years ago, 'Education cannot compensate for society'. Failing inner city schools are a reflection of failing inner cities. Locally, nationally and internationally, we must address questions of economy, employment and exclusion if we are to create an environment for learning.

For years, teachers have felt blamed for most of the ills of society. England didn't excel at sport? Lazy teachers stopped doing team games. Illegitimate births? Immoral teachers don't teach standards. Shortage of skilled labour? Incompetent teachers. Now, once again, we see signs of the old chestnut: unemployment? Schools are turning out unemployable kids.

This book is an attempt to bite back. I am just one of 400,000 who give their all for the country's young people. Through all the muck and bullets, we carry on, almost always obeying the latest daft order. Collectively, we hold a bank of experience, knowledge and commitment, which is the great ignored resource of our education system. We want to be part of an improving school system, but in the city we have to start from where we really are. The story I tell might seem dismal, but it is the real story.

For this is a teacher's story.

1

FAILING SCHOOL

WHAT FOLLOWS IS THE HEART OF THIS BOOK. It is an attempt to describe the realities of inner city classrooms. Of course, there are many realities. What I wish to convey is the ordinary, the commonplace which will be recognised by inner city teachers, and to some extent their families and friends. It will not be recognised by others; certainly, by policy makers and pontificators. The realities are quite obviously largely unrecognised, because, if they were understood, they would not be allowed to continue. I am avoiding highlighting extreme incidents, because it is precisely the ordinary which is so awful. This is a reflection of the commonly expressed sentiment, found for example in the Elton Report, that major incidents of violence are comparatively uncommon, and that the persistence of petty disruption is the greater problem.

I could have presented this picture in academic form. As a sociologist, I am aware of the form and content of some classroom observation research. However, I shall not discuss at length my theoretical model and methodology. I do not claim this study to be rigorously academic. I have deliberately avoided the use of references and authorities. However, a key question for any research is, can it be replicated? I am confident that what I have seen could be seen by others.

I carried out my observations in different parts of the country in a number of secondary schools generally accepted to be 'difficult' which had failed Ofsted inspections. They were undertaken near the start of the academic year, which as teachers know is one of the less disruptive periods. Had I observed in late November, the temperature would have been higher. I was presented to the classes I observed as a researcher into teaching method. I observed whole lessons in a non-participatory mode. On occasion, I followed up by using informal interview techniques to elicit further information from the class teacher. I observed classes of different ages and ability levels. Of course, my reports must be selections of the thousands of interactions occurring in any one lesson. I have attempted to make the selection representative, the picture fair. Only my peers, the teachers in such schools, can judge whether I have been successful. To those who believe I exaggerate, particularly politicians, I simply say, find out for yourselves. Don't make high profile visits to such schools, and listen to the smoothly misleading headteacher; have your researchers seek the reality of inner city classrooms — and then think on.

Looking at the pupils

Inspectors visit classrooms to focus on the teachers. How have they planned the lessons? How do they execute them? And then, perhaps, how does the class receive them? A central contention of this book is that current official theory about classroom performance distorts the nature of the relationship between pupil and teacher, at least in the kind of school I am describing. An assumption is made that, to put it at its weakest, the teacher is the principal determinant of social relations in the classroom. On this model, pupil responses are produced by the content of the lesson and its style of delivery by the teacher. In a sense, pupils start a lesson as empty vessels, to be filled with a fluid which, with a good teacher, will bubble and froth.

The teacher is not my focus. I am looking at the pupils. The simple truth is that a class consists of, say, thirty-one people, of whom one is different from all the others. The one can only be the principal determinant of that group's behaviour if granted that right by the thirty. It is a question, as sociologists say, of the legitimacy of authority. In most schools, most teachers are indeed granted that authority, sometimes won with a struggle, but the current official model seems to assume that this is automatic. It is not. A classroom is socially dynamic, and all its participants bring to it sets of attitudes and behaviour patterns from many sources. If pupils bring to the classroom a refusal to accept the the teacher's authority, then the teacher simply cannot be expected to be able to control them as prescribed by the theory.

In this book, I describe pupils like that. In this chapter, I describe how they behave in school. Where thirty people are in a large room together for an hour, the number of individual social interactions runs into thousands, and there is no technique by which anyone can perceive more than a minority. Like any report, then, the following are selections from the activities in the rooms I observe. My aim is to record the commonplace, the ordinary, the behaviour which sets the tone. The pupils are in the foreground.

The teachers are in the background of these pictures only because I want to keep the focus on the pupils. To interpret these teachers as passive recipients of the pupils' messages would be as ridiculous as the opposite; the teachers are very actively and purposefully attempting to impose their wills on the lessons. What they do is probably not different from what is done by teachers up and down the country. The difference, in these classrooms, is what the pupils do, how they react, the behaviour they bring to the classroom interactions.

The classrooms I describe share one set of characteristics. They are all in schools situated in deprived inner city areas, or on massive estates on the edges of cities. Their intakes are skewed overwhelmingly towards the bottom of our social hierarchy. They are all, coincidentally or not, labelled by the state as 'failing schools'. Let us look through some of the windows — but be quiet, because no-one will want us to see.

On the staircase

It's a secondary school. The corridors and staircases seem dark, the drab colours of the paintwork unrelieved by decoration. This is not due to staff laziness, but the knowledge that anything on the walls here would be defaced and destroyed almost immediately and routinely. The bell sounds for a change of lessons.

A group of Year 8 pupils emerges from a classroom onto the corridor. This class is noteworthy because it has just been with one of the strongest members of staff in the school. The class had been quiet and orderly. The pupils do not rush out, but walk out quietly. In the corridor, they mix with another group emerging from the next classroom. Their task is to go through the swing doors, down two flights of stairs, through another set of doors, and along another corridor to their next lessons. This task will occupy ten minutes.

The staircase is where sixty young people going down meet sixty young people coming up. In this school, that will always be an event. On this occasion, verbal banter gets out of hand; friends meet, stop, and discuss tonight while blocking movement; someone on the top landing spits on those below, perhaps aiming at someone, perhaps aimlessly; others show their disgust by retaliating in kind; pushing and shoving starts. All the time, a trickle of pupils moves up and down, whilst a large number of pupils just hover. And all the time, the noise levels rise, with multiple conversations, shouted arrangements, complaints.

Then, the strong man head of department, having supervised his class out of his room, and hurriedly checked his materials for the next lesson, appears at the stop of the stairs. He speaks. I know this because I see his mouth move. He can be heard only by those close to him. If he shouted with all his considerable force, he might be heard by all, but it would have little impact on the crowd. He knows this because it is a daily scene, and he has tried all kinds of tactics on his staircase to control it — without success.

So, step by step, and group by group, he calmly insists on the pupils moving on to their lesson. Many of them appear to resent this: but it is difficult to know whether they genuinely resent it, and if so, why, or whether this is one more piece of display. In any case, it may take some persuasion before all but the most recalcitrant have moved, and the strong man must return to his room and the now waiting class. Those moving away will reach the downstairs corridor. Will they reach their destination classrooms? Eventually. Well, most of them. If their next lesson is particularly unattractive, some will wander the school, or make themselves unobtrusive in some corner, or perhaps take a trip to the shops for a while.

This well established and senior member of staff uses all his experience and skill to cajole, there is no better word for it, some compliance from pupils. I have seen young teachers, with little experience or status within the school, try and very largely fail in the same situation. No wonder many staff will wait in their rooms for their pupils to arrive. A large proportion of the incidents in this school which involve teachers being sworn at, jostled, pushed, or punched, occur in the corridors.

At those moments in which the teachers must make split second decisions about how to deal with difficult problems of crowd control, at the front of their minds is the knowledge that retaliation for any verbal or physical assault will be regarded as unacceptable. As I write these words, I have just had reported a routine affair in a similar school. A young teacher obstructed the unauthorised exit of a pupil from his classroom by standing in front of the door. She simply punched him and slipped past. This young person has been permanently excluded from two other schools for violence against staff, but the head of this failing school — she was bound to end up there — is refusing to do the same because the punch was the teacher's own fault; he had acted provocatively.

I know that the school improvers will be already fidgeting, their hands up. Other schools have addressed these problems of movement and order in the public spaces. Here is a list of strategies. Yes, yes, yes. Let me discuss some of them later. My point here is that the failing school suffers the problem with a qualitatively different degree and frequency. The problem in the school I describe has changed shape little over twenty or thirty years, through changes of staff and management, and despite repeated attempts to address the problem using a variety of ideas.

Eventually, however, most of the pupils are in their classrooms. Or, at least, in a classroom. It is by no means infrequent that pupils will attend their lesson of choice, rather than one assigned to them by the timetable. They prefer to stick with their friends, and if their friends are in a class with a new teacher, or a supply teacher, as is common, they can offer false names and carry on socialising.

The French class

A Year 9 French class is beginning. The pupils wander in, in dribs and drabs, and sit round tables in groups of four to six. There are twenty of them. They chat amongst themselves. Five minutes after the bell, the teacher, who is just beginning her second year in the career, starts to call the register. The pupils continue to chat. Some answer their names, some answer at the second call. Nine minutes after the bell, the last pupil arrives, saying she is late because she went home for dinner.

While taking the register, the teacher asks Alison to sit down (she is across the room from her place, talking to a group of girls).

'Oh, just one sec,' replies Alison, with a slight note of annoyance that she has been disturbed. Alison does not sit down. Victoria, on the other hand, with her booted feet on the table, has been joining in the same conversation from across the room.

'Victoria, put your feet down and stop talking, please,' says the teacher. There is no pause in the conversation, no indication that Victoria has heard the teacher. Even though the buzz of conversation remains loud, she must have heard. The teacher decides to ignore this, in order to start the learning activity. She asks for attention. There is a slight reduction in noise level. She tells the class she will write numbers on the board, and the class must say them in French. Most pupils carry on talking, but six pay attention. One or two call out the answers. Someone turns on the large tape recorder standing on a bench at the side, and a loud German voice is heard, but the nearest pupil turns it off when asked by the teacher. With the class not responding to the activity, the teacher tries a different tack.

'When I say your name, tell me the French for the number I point to.' She continues to speak in a calm way, without raising her voice, and it seems unlikely that many pupils would have heard it above the noise of the conversations continuing around the room. Yet when she calls out, 'John,' he turns from his neighbour, says 'vingt-quatre,' and turns back again. Calling a series of names in quick succession, the response is the correct answer, either from the pupil called, or from two or three others. Meanwhile, at the table where Alison, Victoria and four others are sitting, there is a discussion about the new fifty pence coin.

'Oi, miss,' calls out Tracey, 'how long can we use the old fifty pences?'

'We're not talking about fifty pences, we're supposed to be saying numbers in French,' replies the teacher and writes the name Tracey on the board.

'Oi, Tracey, she's written your name up,' says Alison. 'Hey, miss, that ain't fair, I ain't done nothing,' says Tracey. They continue the chat, the teacher asks a few more pupils. Across the room, four boys are discussing whether the transfer of Teddy Sheringham has proved a success.

'We'll do some written work now,' says the teacher, and starts to give out a pile of folders, explaining the task as she goes. The class continues to chat, but somehow absorbs the instructions, because after a few minutes fidgeting, borrowing pens, checking what has to be done, most of the pupils are copying from the board the drawings of the clocks, and writing down how to say the time.

That is not to say the room goes quiet. Most groups are still talking, and the group containing Alison, Victoria and Tracey takes the opportunity to become a little bit louder, while ostentatiously pushing their folders away, unopened. After unavailing requests, the teacher writes the names of Victoria and Jane on the board, but when she goes to the far corner of the room to guide some boys on the work, Steven slips from his place, erases the names, and returns silently and unnoticed. Steven, who has been sitting by himself idly doodling on scraps of paper that came to hand, receives little thanks.

Alison shouts across the room, 'Steven, you wanker, when we want your help we'll ask for it.' Steven does not respond.

Continuing at some volume, Alison says, apparently to Jane, 'He's a skanky twat. 'Ere, have you seen his trainers? 'E's got the same ones as Smigger,' and the girls on their table laugh.

Victoria calls out, 'Oi, you big skank, where d'ya get your trainers?' Steven, head down, carries on doodling, while some others call out, 'Fight fight fight fight,' but arouse no interest.

'Why are you in this class? No-one likes you,' continues Victoria, but the lack of response either from the unfortunate Steven or from the rest of the class apparently discourages her group from developing the action, and they turn to other diversions. Meanwhile, the teacher has finished working with the group at the far table, and returns to the centre of the room, asking the class to get on with the work. Most appear to be doing so, while maintaining their conversations.

Not, however, the disruptive girls group. They start playing the forfeit game, Spin the Pencil. The pencil spins and points to Jane. She spins it again, and it points at Alison. There is some banter about what the forfeit might be, but in the end, Jane tells Alison she must go round the room as a lesbian. Alison gets up, clearly unsure of how to present the role, but makes for another table of girls. Just as she starts to say, 'Hello, darling…', the teacher says, 'Alison, go back to your place, now, please,' and Alison does so. She has attracted little interest from her classmates. She spins the pencil again; it points at Jane.

Victoria says, 'I know, kiss Tessa's boobs.'

'No, that's crude… I know, go over to David and say, "David, I love you, we've been together so long, will you marry me?"'

Jane shows no interest in carrying out this forfeit, so after some more chat the game ends. While it has been continuing, the teacher has ignored it, while encouraging others to do the work set, moving around the tables. While the level of conversation continues, most of the other pupils are making some kind of attempt, although they are distracted from time to time either by comments from others on their own table, or by the performance of the disruptive girls. One boy is occupied in tearing a piece of exercise paper into ever smaller fragments, though he does not appear to be making pellets for immediate use. One of the girls throws a pen across the room. Someone retrieves it and throws it back. Four of the disruptive girls start to sing, quite loudly, the chorus of *When I'm Sixty-Four*, but it peters out.

The lesson moves towards its close. Those who have been attempting the work, in an offhand way, are losing their concentration, and events gain speed. Someone finds a conker, and throws that across the room. Naturally, it is returned. The boy who has been tearing paper has now used another sheet to make a paper aeroplane. He gives it a test flight. He leaves his place to recover the plane. As he moves across the room, he picks up a pen from a table, and throws it out of the window.

Someone shouts,

'Miss, someone threw my pen outta the window.' The teacher asks who did it.

'It was me,' answers the perpetrator cheerfully. 'I'll go down and get it.'

He leaves the room. This seems to give a girl an idea, because she also gets up and goes out of the room. She opens the door to the classroom opposite, and has a conversation with someone in that room.

Simultaneously, Steven, who has continued to doodle in a miserable way, receives some abuse and the six girls start the shout, 'Cry-baby, cry-baby, cry-baby.' Suddenly Alison and Steven are out of their seats, grappling at the front of the room, as many of the pupils shout. The teacher has to grab them and force them to untangle their arms. The conflict is largely ritual, with no blows struck or injuries caused, but Steven grabs his jacket and rushes out of the room.

There are still five minutes before the bell. A number of pupils stand up, put on jackets, and make their way to the door. The teacher comes across, stands in front of the door, and instructs the pupils to go back and sit down. They retreat a pace. Someone turns on the recorder again at full blast, this time finding music.

'Turn that off,' demands the teacher, but when a girl tries to do so a boy brushes away her hand, and the noise continues. Pupils mill around the room, but the teacher says loudly, 'I shall not dismiss the class until everyone is sitting down.'

As some do, the bell goes.

'Everyone sit down,' commands the teacher. They do. When everyone is seated, Alison gets up, stands right in front of the teacher who is at the door, and says, 'May I leave, please?'

'No, sit down like the others.'

'May I leave please. May I leave please. May I leave please. May I leave please.'

The teachers response is drowned out by the repetition. Eventually, she stands aside and Alison does, indeed, leave. The teacher then tells the class that the behaviour has been unacceptable, that she will follow it up, and that there will be consequences. Then she dismisses the class and the pupils leave, quietly.

The drama class

I meet the drama teacher outside the classroom. It's the first few weeks of her career.

'We've got to come here because a window is being repaired in the hall where I usually do lessons, so I've prepared a theory lesson.'

As the Year 8 pupils come up the stairs and through the doors, there is a problem. There appears to be a Year 11 group already in the room.

'I'm in here — would you like to use the studio?' suggests a colleague.

'Right, 8DP, make your way quietly and sensibly to the studio.' And under her breath, to me: 'Oh, God, they'll be wound up like springs after this.'

As we reach the studio, the pupils are milling around.

'Line up against that wall.'

Most do, some hover.

'When you go in, take a chair and sit in a circle.'

As we enter, about half a dozen boys are picking up chairs and throwing them across the huge room, measuring about sixty feet square.

'Stop that at once. Sit round in a circle,' calls out the teacher.

She sits down, calls the register. Twenty-two of the twenty-four pupils in the group are in school, but three boys have not come into the studio. Two more are running round while the register is being called. The teacher goes outside, finds the missing ones, and brings them in. She goes back to the circle, and explains the task. Some talking continues, and once or twice pupils call out across the circle. The pupils are asked to work in their groups.

One of the groups moves to the terracing, sits down, and discusses the task.

For the rest, all is movement and noise. Some pupils chase each other round the studio. Some pull the large curtains at the end, and disappear behind them. Some run outside, and back in. There is calling out, loud talking. A girl screeches at another. The teacher moves around, talking to groups and individuals. After a few minutes she calls them to sit on the circle of chairs. About half do so, and the teacher intercepts others and instructs them to sit down. Gradually, taking three minutes, they all sit down.

Ignoring the inappropriate behaviour, the teacher asks them to report back. She emphasises the work of one group which has completed the task, and introduces the next activity. Raising her voice to compete with the large space in the studio and three other conversations, she explains what is required. As she continues, the other conversations drop. With a reminder on their behaviour, she completes her instruction and asks them to break up into groups again.

This is a signal for more of the same. Some boys break into a play fight. Others jump up onto staging and jump off. Some run outside again. The teacher calls them together again. Most sit down on the terracing, but some remain moving around. Without appearing to lose self-control, the teacher speaks loudly and forcibly.

'8DP, you are totally embarrassing. In front of a visitor, you have to let yourselves down. You have a small change in your routine and you go to pieces. Now I want you to settle down to finish your plans in the next ten minutes, and stop being such an embarrassment.'

More movement, but within a couple of minutes three groups, containing eleven pupils, are sitting talking quietly. Only one, however, appears to be dealing with the task set. The other pupils are still standing up, and a few still run round and round, chasing each other. The teacher calls them to put their chairs away, and give in their planning sheets. Most do so. The bell goes, and she dismisses them.

The teacher kneels on the floor to gather up some dropped planning sheets. She bursts into tears.

The English class

The Year 10 English group has thirteen pupils present. The teacher, the head of department, has just joined the school. As they came in, they are given a sheet with a word search, are sat down and instructed to start it. Within a couple of minutes, the teacher asks a boy to move to another place on his own, and after a grumble he does so. Almost all the pupils are trying the task, with some quiet conversation.

The teacher calls the register, and corrects each respondent until she receives the answer she expects. She then explains that she has started the group with a simple exercise, which she expects to be finished soon, and then they will move on to more brain-taxing activity. She gives the instructions for the second and third activities of the lesson.

Jason and Lance sit together at the back of the room. They are not on task. They mostly talk to each other. Occasionally they lean forward to attract the attention of Joe or Matthew, sitting in front of them, or Michelle, sitting next to them. When he thinks the teacher is not looking, Jason spits out of the open first floor window. Lance is fidgeting with felt-tip pens. He tends to break into a few lines of pop songs, in a quiet way. After a while, the teacher calls for Lance.

'Come and do a job for me,' she says, and they disappear into a stock cupboard just outside the room. Lance returns carrying a pile of books which he gives out. The teacher reminds the class that they should be moving onto the second activity, and reminds Jason and Lance that she expects to see some work done by the end of the lesson. After a while, eight of the pupils are working steadily, Joe and Matthew are working sporadically, Michelle is working occasionally, and Jason and Lance do no work at all. The teacher praises those who are on task, and intervenes with the others. She persuades Joe and Matthew to move, thus largely isolating Jason and Lance.

A wasp flies through the window. Jason makes great play of swatting it, while Lance prepares a swatter by rolling up his exercise book. Lance chases the wasp round the room, joined by another boy. Gently the teacher suggests that if they leave it alone it will go away, but the chase is too exciting. Most pupils are disturbed by this but do not join in; they simply watch the action. Eventually the wasp escapes, and order is restored. The teacher continues to move from table to table, checking on progress. On reaching Jason and Lance, she firmly says she expects to see something completed by the end of the lesson. Shortly afterwards, Lance wanders round the room, apparently hoping to 'borrow' some answers, but returns to his table when instructed.

The scene is apparently calm, with a low level of noise from conversations between partners at tables, and more people working than not. As the lesson moves into its final third, however, the calm starts to be put under pressure. As the teacher moves past a table, she pushes a bag from the gangway further under the table. There is a sharp reaction from James.

'Don't touch my bag.'

'I was just pushing it out of the way.'

'Don't touch my bag, alright, just don't touch my bag.'

'James, all I did…'

'I said, don't touch my bag. Do I touch your handbag? Do I? Do I touch your handbag?'

'James, there's no need to talk...'

'Do I touch your handbag, though, do I? Do I? Do I?'

The teacher moves away, towards the other side of the room, saying, 'Don't be rude, James... James... James,' and the exchange ends.

Shortly afterwards, a paper pellet is flicked across the room from the direction of Joe and Matthew. It comes back. Other small objects traverse the room, with accompanying complaints, protestations of innocence, and swearing. The teacher moves in to separate Joe and Matthew. They move to their allotted places with little complaint, but they no longer pretend to do more work. Awaiting her chance, Michelle slips Lance her answers, which he copies into his book. The teacher continues to move gently round the tables, guiding and cajoling, but she has little co-operation when she reaches Jason and Lance. Annoyed at something he is told by Michelle, Lance calls across the room, 'Oi, Rachel, you little scab...' but is sharply interrupted by the teacher. Her opinion that such is an inappropriate use of language is accepted by Lance.

With five minutes to go, the class automatically moves into finishing the lesson, with little resistance from the teacher. When the bell goes, the teacher dismisses the class name by name, leaving Joe, Jason and Lance. She closes the classroom door. A girl from another group opens it from outside. The teacher closes it again. One of the other boys in the group opens it from the outside. The teacher closes it again.

'I'm going, miss,' says Jason. The teacher ignores this, talking to Joe about a detention he had missed. Joe agrees to do it tonight, but as they complete the conversation Jason walks out. Joe is dismissed, and the teacher asks Lance about his work. Lance becomes discomfited, gets up, and starts to walk away. The teacher tells him that he and Jason will be separated from now on, just as Lance walks out of the room.

The teacher has stayed calm throughout. 'There's no point in getting worked up,' she tells me. 'I know that if I just keep plugging away, I'll get there in the end.'

The maths class

Twelve pupils are present in the Year 11 maths class. Ten minutes after the pips, the teacher has made sure every pupil has a text book, an exercise book and has heard the instructions for the lesson, and he is circulating to check that everyone is on task. A boy and a girl, each sitting alone at the front of the class, are on task. The others are not. Malcolm sits with his feet on a chair, leaning against the wall, wearing earphones. Janice stands on desktops, pulling open the blinds and letting in the bright sunlight. Miriam follows on behind, pulling them closed again. Two girls sit together, chatting. Three boys are listening to the teacher explaining again how to work the number machine.

He completes the explanation again with a quiet exhortation to do the work, and turns to ask Malcolm to take off the earphones. Malcolm does so.

'I need to go to the toilet,' he says in a desultory and unconvincing tone. He is ignored. Miriam has sat with the two girls, and they chat on, although they are holding pens as if they intend to make some entries in their exercise books. The teacher sits with them, checking they are able to do the work, and encouraging them. He moves on to the working loner.

The room seems calm, with small groups of young people sitting talking quietly. The teacher cannot, however, persuade them to do the work set. The groups he has coached have made no real effort after he moved on. The boy at the front has stopped, too, and starts looking at a magazine. Then Malcolm calls out, more loudly than before,

'Can I go to the toilet, sir?'

'No' is the immediate calm reply as sir continues helping the girl at the front. Malcolm then nudges Janice, who has sat down at the table behind him.

'Fuck off you little dickhead,' she responds sharply.

'Mind your language,' observes the teacher in the same calm tone. Janice gets up and goes to join the group of three.

'Why come over here?' one says. 'It was peaceful.'

'Am I going to talk to you?' says Janice.

One of the boys helped earlier in the lesson calls out,

'Sir, d'you know how long I've been waiting? Haven't you heard me calling you?'

'Funny how you never hear me when I speak to you,' says the teacher. He comes back to the boy's table, and explains something again. They also have a good natured conversation about a school sports event. The teacher moves on. Another one of the four says, quietly,

'I can't fucking do this,' and puts on some earphones. The boy at the front doodles, then gets out a calculator and plays with it.

The classroom door opens, and a girl stands there. Three people call out to her, and abrasive conversations ensue.

'Sir, can I borrow a ruler?' she asks. The teacher finishes his work with a pupil, goes to a cupboard, and gives her a ruler. She leaves. Another girl gets up from her place, sits on the table in front of Malcolm, and starts a conversation with him.

'Get on with your work, Jackie,' says the teacher.

'Sir, I'm talking to Malcolm.'

'That's what I'm worried about.' Jackie continues to talk to Malcolm.

The teacher continues to circulate, advising, persuading, calmly requesting the pupils to do the work. Only one pupil, the girl at the front, is working steadily. The lesson drones on.

The Spanish class

Ten pupils wander into the room for the Year 10 Spanish lesson. They spread themselves in ones and twos around the room. Instructions are on the board. The first task is to copy some words in Spanish and English from a sheet into exercise books. They open their books. It is ten minutes since the pips went to indicate the change of lessons. Denise, sitting alone at the back of the room, starts working. No-one else does.

Nineteen minutes after the pips, the door is thrown open and two boys walk in. One, Daniel, approaches Denise and starts a conversation, the other sits down. The teacher persuades Daniel to sit down, and sets about explaining to them the tasks. Daniel, however, is talking to three boys at the next table. 'Daniel, Daniel, Daniel,' repeats the teacher softly, but Daniel does not acknowledge him or respond. The teacher gives the instructions anyway.

Then two of the three get up and ask the teacher for a note to go somewhere. The teacher decides the journey is unnecessary, and the boys resume their seats, and resume their conversation about computer games. Soon, Shaun leaves this conversation and wanders over to Denise. He sits down next to her and they chat, while she carries on working. A boy sitting on his own in another corner of the room is also working. Another boy comes over and sits on a table to join the computer games conversation.

As the chat continues, the teacher quietly circulates, persuading pupils to do the work and checking their progress. Shaun has started copying some answers from Denise's book as they talk, but when the teacher comes to their table, Shaun moves back to his place.

A boy gets up and walks out of the room. No reason is apparent. Shortly afterwards he returns.

Dean has got out a computer games magazine, and is flicking through it while joining the conversation. He is also talking across the room to Daniel. Although the room still seems calm, there is an edge to this conversation. Suddenly, Daniel's voice is raised.

'You're a cow and a bitch,' he shouts at Dean, and rushes across the room at him. He grabs hold of the magazine and a tug-of-war develops.

'Le'go, le'go, le'go, you bastard,' shouts Daniel, whilst other boys also shout. Inevitably, the magazine tears, and Daniel goes back to his place with some of the pages. Shaun shouts,

'Daniel, you wanker, you owe me ten pound.'

'I ain't gonna give you no ten pound.'

'You fucking t'ief.'

The excitement dies down. Daniel turns to a boy who has not been involved:

'What's wrong wiv you man, you stink. Oi, who's farted?'

After a short pause, the edge develops again as Daniel and Dean swap insults across the room.

'You stupid gay.'

'You stupid smelly fool.' Dean moves towards the teacher, asking for support. He says,

'He gives me stress.'

The teacher replies,

'You give him stress,' and asks everyone to calm down. The two continue.

'Shutup.'

'Shutup yourself.'

'Bighead.'

'You're the one with the big features.'

This comment attracts general laughter around the room.

'Ugly monkey.'

Soon, the altercation ends, and the room resumes a strained calm. The teacher has another conversation with Dean about winding up other people. Two other boys are discussing ways to leave the school premises. One reveals that the lock on the back gate is bust, allowing a surreptitious departure.

'This school's a shithole,' they agree.

Still circulating, the teacher reaches Denise again. Denise strikes up a conversation about the lack of equity in the school rules on smoking. Her main thesis is that half the teachers smoke, so why shouldn't the pupils. After some inconclusive debate, Denise says that she has finished her work, and what is she supposed to do now? With just over five minutes left, they agree there is no point in starting anything new. Two boys who have been doing the colouring task have also finished, and join Dean who is still looking at the magazine.

With five minutes to go, and without any signal from the teacher, the class starts to clear up. One boy collects in the text books, others pack their bags. Daniel and Dean continue their abrasive relationship. As the pips go, most of the pupils leave quietly. A couple of boys, still looking at the magazine, are in no hurry.

Afterwards, the teacher tells me, 'I'm sitting on a bombshell. You never know when it's going to go off.'

He explains some technicalities of language learning, and points out how difficult it is to get these pupils beyond the initial stage. His priority is to keep the class calm, and to try to prevent the most difficult pupils from winding up each other.

The mission impossible

These lessons were selected at random. Four of the five, in different schools, with a range of age groups and subjects, were very similar. The fifth, the drama lesson, was very different. It had a number of factors which enhanced the difficulty of producing an orderly lesson. The group was faced initially with a change of routine. It was required to travel across the school to a different venue, which was bound to prevent a snappy start to the lesson. The room was completely unsuitable, being large enough to invite movement. The teacher was new to the school, and was still learning its style, as well as getting to know the individual pupils. The teacher was also in the first few weeks of her career, and was learning the realities of the craft and the necessary coping mechanisms.

The government's strategy for improving achievement in these schools rests on the assumption that low achievement is caused by poor teaching. What better teaching techniques could have led to a different outcome for this lesson? A key moment was the entry of the group to the studio. The pupils had been lined up against a wall in order to settle them down prior to entry. Fine judgements are involved in this technique; it is not uncommon to find two or three who cannot or will not stand still and silent, but if efforts to gain their compliance take too long, the twenty others will become restless. It is preferable, of course, for the teacher to be in the room before the pupils arrive, so that as they enter they can be guided immediately to an activity. However, that is not always possible, as in this case. My judgement was that the teacher handled this phase appropriately.

The next critical decision was where the teacher would position herself in relation to the class as it entered the studio. As so often, she was defeated by her incapacity to be in a number of places simultaneously. She waited at the entrance to ensure that all the pupils entered, rather than disappearing down the corridor, but felt obliged to go in when the first pupils inside started throwing chairs. Sure enough, the stragglers took advantage of this by not coming into the room. Again, had the teacher known in advance where she would be teaching, and had she been given the preparation time, she could have set out the chairs before the pupils arrived; but, as so often, such reasonable conditions did not apply.

The teacher then judged that the best way to restore order was to rely on the quality of the lesson content. This exactly follows the theory of teacher trainers and advisers: a well-planned lesson with appropriate materials and activities will attract the positive attention of the class. She attempted this by getting most of the pupils to sit in the circle, explaining and setting the task, all with the minimum of delay, and without the time-consuming and negative effort of gaining complete attention from all. The aim was to gain some stability by having a core of the pupils engaged positively, and to draw in the remainder.

There were two main reasons for the failure of this strategy. The first is that the size of the room made it impossible to keep in touch with the number of incidents occurring simultaneously, or to intervene effectively with each of them, or to prevent pupils running out of it. The second is that there was no core of engaged pupils. Only one group consistently attended to the task set. It was not that the lesson content was poor; to me, a non-specialist, it should have been appealing to a Year 8 class, but it was obvious that, far from rejecting the work as boring, the large majority of the class never seriously considered it. It is worth noting that a few weeks after this lesson, this teacher received an extremely positive report from a specialist inspector.

It is not easy, then, to identify what the teacher did wrong, and I do not know what other techniques could have been successful in the circumstances. The inescapable conclusion is that the responsibility lies with the pupils. In essence, they refused to comply with reasonable instructions. Individually and collectively, they decided to ignore their teacher and to play in whatever ways they chose. A school, like any other social institution, has standard patterns of behaviour which are subject to general consent. In this example, consent was unilaterally withdrawn. The only argument left to those who would wish to put all responsibility with the teachers is that this one must have been inadequate personally, if she did not carry sufficient authority to ensure compliance. Let us examine the other lessons observed before returning to this argument.

Teaching by the three Cs

The English, Maths and Spanish lessons exhibited great similarities. The atmosphere was generally calm, with a quiet buzz of conversation. The French lesson, with a teacher less experienced than the other three, was more rowdy. In each case, there were potentially explosive incidents of conflict between pupils, with physical grappling in two of the classes, although no major incidents ensued.

At the same time, there was an edge to the atmosphere in each room. The overall impression was of truce between teacher and pupils, rather than peace, or, less still, partnership. The demeanour of the pupils was one of indifference to the official purpose of schooling. There was a lack of connection between the two sides. This separation was not complete. Most pupils had the relevant books open in front of them, perhaps held pens in their hands throughout the lessons. Many did parts of the work set as they chatted. Others took the trouble to copy some of the answers from their classmates. In every lesson, a few appeared to concentrate on the task for all or most of the time, but for the majority, these actions were concessions to the teacher.

On the other hand, there were many actions signifying a claim for autonomy on the part of pupils. There were examples of inappropriate language, ignoring the teacher when being spoken to, moving round, or out of, the room at will, and a general atmosphere of talk and activity unconnected with the lesson. For the French teacher, this was clearly the site of a struggle, as each side sought to impose its will. Although she remained outwardly calm throughout, this was a tense classroom. The other three, to varying degrees, felt as if an accommodation had been reached. For the sake of peace, each side had in effect made concessions. There are few social institutions in which leaders can exert power without any regard for the led, and in schools authority is only granted conditionally to the teacher. However, in the observed classrooms it is difficult to describe the position of the teacher as one of authority. There is, indeed, a truce between opposed parties, that is sometimes stretched to the limits because there is no commonality of goal.

The structure of all the lessons consisted of an initial instruction either displayed on the board, or given orally by the teacher, or both, with the teacher then circulating between groups of pupils checking progress, and giving help and encouragement. There was no attempt at class teaching, in the form of either a teacher monologue or question and answer. Minor offences were frequently ignored, with teachers making dozens of judgements on whether to ignore them, or whether to risk a breach of the truce by pursuing them. These judgements involved calculation of the likelihood of any situation escalating into something that could not be ignored.

In each of the lessons except French, the truce was exemplified by the ending, in which pupils decided when it was time to pack away, did so with implied permission, and waited quietly for the bell which was their signal to leave. Tension was created in the English lesson when the teacher detained some pupils after that time, in an attempt both to counsel them, and also to alter the authority gradient. This was resisted by the pupils walking out, but this teacher would continue to push gently to reduce pupil autonomy.

A feature of all the lessons was the negative relationships between some pupils, which was the main source of disorder. Apparently light-hearted banter could escalate within seconds into real anger and aggression, and pupils would not accept arbitration from the teacher. On the basis of single lesson observations, it is impossible to know the antecedents of any of these incidents, but in my experience it is very difficult for the class teacher to predict them. Friends become enemies very quickly and with little cause, enemies resort to violence easily, and may well become friends again very soon. It is very likely that Dean, whose magazine was torn by Daniel in the Spanish lesson, will have retaliated with interest, and perhaps some other teacher will have been the unlucky person *in loco parentis* at that moment.

Once again, the experts are here already at their word processors. They will be unable to resist explaining just how the teaching and learning in these classrooms could be improved by this, that, and the other strategy. No doubt, most experienced teachers could pick on some elements of these classrooms and explain how things could be done better. The experts will be saying more than that. No doubt they will notice the simple tasks being given in most of the lessons. What these youngsters need, they will say, is more stimulating and challenging work. The reason such methods are not being used in these schools is that they do not work.

What the experts do not realise is that a significant proportion of the pupils in these classes resent being stimulated and refuse to take up a challenge. This assertion will be condemned by many experts, and the proponents of the can-do culture, as being unjustifiably negative. Their explanation for classrooms like those I have described is that the teachers are not good enough. I suggest that this explanation is unlikely and incorrect, and offer an alternative.

It is not an accident that the teachers observed had similar approaches, based on what I describe later as the three 3Cs: cajolery, compromise, and conciliation. They used similar methods because they were reacting to similar circumstances. None of these teachers were regarded by their managers or inspectors as incompetent, despite their schools being under the closest of scrutiny. Three of them had taught successfully in other schools. What none of them could do was to ensure that the pupils all completed the tasks set, even less that they learnt anything significant. This is not to say they had given up, or that they did not wish their pupils to be successful. In their classrooms, they were doing what was possible. These teachers are under a most intense scrutiny, and under incredible pressure to 'improve'. They receive 'support' and 'training' with great frequency. Yet, in all the circumstances, they could not force the pupils to do more; greater pressure would meet greater resistance, and conflict which would be unlikely to be resolved in favour of the teacher.

Now it is just possible, I suppose, that all the most incompetent teachers in the country, by some grotesque mischance, should have assembled themselves in these schools; perhaps it is some sophisticated conspiracy against the nation's poor. If that explanation does not appeal, we are forced to look elsewhere to understand why these teachers are unable to obtain compliant and achieving classrooms. The key is that a teaching strategy and style which would be effective in most schools in the country, which would produce satisfactory pupil performance and the approval of the inspectors, just will not work in the school for the underclass.

As we have seen, in these schools pupils on occasion break the truce with behaviour which must be resisted. Such confrontations, apart from the killing stress, are negative because they produce a further deterioration in the pupil-teacher relationship and in the overall learning environment. For these pupils there is no reward or sanction powerful enough to overcome a disposition not to co-operate.

The experts will pontificate with a wide variety of advice, but in this country there is no organised body of knowledge about teaching strategies for difficult classes, there is no standard training, and there is no cadre of specialists to act as role models. Australian teachers who migrate to schools in London have benefited from training in classroom control — and it shows. This is why the advisers, task teams, projects and inspectors with their bright ideas for better teaching are not that much help in these classes, and why we need to be more realistic about the school in the inner city.

What is the problem?

One form of realism would be to stop confusing the problem itself with attempts to cope with it. The argument of this book is that in schools for the underclass, ordinary teachers are placed in an extraordinary situation. For too long, the focus — and the condemnation — has centred on the teachers; we need to look again at the situation. We must not mistake the problem for reactions to the problem. The attitudes, manners and behaviour of young people are not created by schools. *They are created by society*, by the communities in which they grow up. Yes, of course schools play a part. I would not be a teacher if I did not think I could play a part. Yet it is a very small part, in comparison with the influences from outside.

What teachers do is to try to cope with those behaviours, manners and attitudes. Those who do not like what they see of young people should not look at the school as part of the problem. Just like all the other agents of the state, teachers are reacting to what is there, not making it. Those who do not like the ways some young people behave in school should not assume that the behaviour is either produced or condoned by the teachers, who after all have to deal with it and suffer its consequences.

Teachers should not be condemned if, like police officers, the judicial system, the social work system, political and economic institutions, they are not completely successful in altering young people. Teachers try, they succeed with some, they fail with others. Should we condemn the teacher described above who could not prevent her pupils from running round the unsuitable setting she found herself in? Or should we condemn the pupils who, as independent agents capable of decision, decided to act in such unreasonable ways? Or, perhaps, we should condemn neither; rather, perhaps we should try to understand a little more, and base our economic and social policies on the understanding.

I have described these classrooms in the hope that readers will gain a rather more realistic view of what goes on in the secondary schools in our inner cities, and a greater determination that appropriate action to deal with the situation is not limited to sacking incompetent teachers. We need to focus a little more on the young people, and a little less on the school, if we are to improve educational attainment in this country.

Aggression in the air

In the most extreme of our schools, the threat of violence often underlies the opposition and tendency to confrontation. It rarely becomes reality because staff learn to avoid confrontation. They are in exactly the same position as other public servants, such as staff in hospital casualty departments, public transport, or housing and DSS offices.

Recently, I witnessed an altercation between a train passenger and a ticket inspector. When challenged for their tickets by the two inspectors, four youths had brushed them aside and run off the train at the next station. The passenger was annoyed that they had been allowed to get away with it, whilst meeker persons who had no fraudulent intent were harassed by inspectors. The inspector pointed out that following injuries to their colleagues, management had trained them not to attempt to restrain fare dodgers.

Now, teachers are aware of their difficult legal position with regard to physical contact. A recent change in the law has not yet produced any change of attitude or performance; the fact is that if they use any physical restraint on any but the youngest child, disciplinary action is very likely, even if legal action is rare. So avoidance of confrontation is *de rigueur* in schools, just as much as on public transport.

The problem with this approach is that confrontation is just what is sought by the pupils. It is the way they have learnt to resolve tensions. For many of them, all social relations are essentially suspicious, defensive, and prone to confrontations. The image is of one side in an aggressive advance, with the other side preventing a blow by retreating as quickly as necessary, with the occasional side-step for variation.

Hence the rarity of assaults on teachers. The commonest is pushing, when pupils can no longer tolerate the refusal of the teacher to become provoked, and have to leave the scene. Pushing is hardly ever regarded by teachers as an assault, unless the force knocks them over and injures them. Sometimes, of course, the teacher will become provoked, and consider that physical restraint is necessary. Stronger pushing or clench-fisted blows are the common response by the pupil to such restraint, but are not treated as assault because the teacher is regarded as being at fault in making physical contact with the pupil.

Sometimes, the older pupil will take it out on the teacher later by property assault. Typically, this will take the form of an attack on the paintwork or tyres of the teacher's car. Only rarely will the pupil use premeditated violence on the teacher.

In almost every case, the weapons brought into school are intended for use against other pupils, or for general self-defence. Research suggests that as many as one in five do this, and although the teacher is rarely if ever the target, the implied threat increases the stress. When one pupil attacks another with a knife, it is the teacher who has the duty of care.

The day after one such event in a south London school, the head of the neighbouring school thought it would be a good day for one of his occasional searches for weapons. One boy was found in possession of a crowbar. Although knives of various kinds are very often carried, they are not often visible to staff. However, the police confiscate items ranging from penknives to machetes with twelve inch blades from school pupils. The problem for the future is that the rage which currently produces the push will increasingly produce a knife.

The management of the few assaults which do occur is often inadequate. Except in some special schools, teachers receive no training or guidance in dealing with them, and the victims receive little or no support. Instead of being sent home to recuperate, offered stress counselling, compensation for damage to property, and support in legal action, schools typically wish to return to normality with minimum fuss, and offer no support of any kind. It is unusual for the victim even to be relieved of teaching duties. Managers generally give the impression that the teacher is a guilty party for allowing a problem to escalate to violence. With many parents vociferously adopting the same attitude, governing bodies increasingly refuse to exclude pupils who have attacked teachers.

I can remember, as a young teacher, sitting in a staff room in northern England and listening to colleagues recount stories of what amounted to unprovoked physical assault, often causing actual bodily harm, by teachers against young people for minor infringements of rules. No-one wants to return to scenes such as those. However, the pendulum has swung too far.

Rules and procedures have to be made and implemented for reasonable people in reasonable circumstances. As I shall show, it is not reasonable to expect any human being to withstand the incessant provocation that is currently the rule in many of our classrooms. Only saints could turn the other cheek to the extent now demanded. What is needed is an approach to assaults on staff which recognises the reality.

Whether or not the teacher touches the pupil, the cause of such an assault is the behaviour of the pupil, not the reaction of the teacher. Sensible means of supporting the assaulted teacher and punishing the assailant are a vital component in improving inner city schools. As I said above, actual (as opposed to threatened) physical violence is not the central problem of order in these places. A policy on assaults is just one brick in the wall. Rather, the picture is one of opposition; unrelenting, unforgiving opposition. It is not simply that the teacher is obstructed; the teacher, and learning, are marginalised in the classrooms described here.

Of course, there are few classes where every single pupil is a committed opponent of state education. Attitudes vary; for example, most refugee children will be from families which hope that education will be the route to a better life. There will be many working class children whose parents share something of the same attitude. Such children may even form the majority; but, almost by definition, it will be a silent majority. For they will see the role of pupil as involving reasonable compliance; they will sit and wait quietly for the lesson to progress. While there is mayhem around them, they will try to get something out of the lesson, even when their peers and the teacher are involved with quite another agenda.

Compliant pupils are, however, not the major influence in the social dynamic of the classroom. They carry no weight with the heavy brigade, and are likely to be in the same fear of their physical well-being as the teacher. They simply sit and watch the classroom action. Some, no doubt, hope that the action keeps going until the bell, so that they will not be forced to display what they regard as their academic inadequacies, while others, hope endlessly that one day they will be able to get on with progressing towards qualifications.

Apart from the pupil mix, there are other variables, of course, in the classroom dynamic, the most important of which is the teacher. Much of the research on the subject suggests that pupils' respect for a teacher is conditional on aspects of the teacher's performance — which seems reasonable. Perceived fairness is a commonly quoted indicator.

However, what such research often misses is the cultural baggage brought into the class by the pupils. As suggested above, even in the most difficult school there will be those who are prepared to accept the teacher's authority, although they may set fairly tough conditions. Yet many children of the underclass reject schooling under any conditions, and their reactions to different teachers simply reflect what they can get away with.

Hence, teachers in these schools need to be extraordinary people. They need the highest level of skill in managing recalcitrant pupils, together with patience and forbearance amounting to stoicism, and some philosophy which justifies their self-inflicted purgatory. They also need a high level of physical fitness and stamina. In fact, they need the same qualities as any successful teacher, but to a greater degree.

Clearly, not all staff in these schools reach these standards. They may be ordinary, not extraordinary people. Clearly, then, the skill of the teacher does make a difference; but it must be understood that disorder does not result from poor teachers, but from groups of pupils who will not respect the authority of *any* teacher — nor, come to that, of any police officer or other authority figure.

At this point, let me repeat that I do not present these descriptions as 'typical' contemporary British classrooms. They represent one end of a continuum, with the sweetly compliant ambition of metroland at the other. And let us remember that the number of internal and external factors which together determine a place on this continuum is very large. But let us finally remind ourselves that, of those factors, the culture brought into school and being remade there is by far the dominant.

Colluding teachers?

Here, I also need to make the statement that these kinds of classrooms are not welcomed by teachers. It will seem ridiculous to my colleagues that it is necessary to say this. Yet one of the silliest current themes, within the discourse which arises from education becoming a high profile political issue, is that somehow teachers conspire in low achievement by their *laisser-faire* attitude to children's behaviour. To see just how silly that is, just imagine what the kinds of scene described above do to teachers.

Facing children whose compliance can never be guaranteed, and indeed frequently breaks down, is in fact the first of two major reasons why teaching is becoming an impossible career in schools for the underclass. It ruins teachers' health. The stress incurred by such work far exceeds that apparently healthy buzz which prepares us for dealing with some difficult task. The stress of facing the kind of class I have described is altogether less positive.

I believe that fear is a more apt word to describe what many teachers feel before they face a class. This is particularly the case in secondary schools. Obviously, but importantly, the clients are larger. In many cases they are larger, heavier and stronger than the teacher. Secondly, they use their physical attributes as part of the threat they make. As I have explained, some secondary school pupils routinely use aggressive and threatening body language against teachers.

Teachers hear reputations, as much as do the pupils. They must deal daily with those convicted of violent crime, members of violent gangs, violent drug dealers, and the like. In reality, many of these young people will try to keep out of trouble with teachers, but their contempt for teachers is always bubbling. The stress for teachers, the fear, is the threat rather than the actuality. It could happen.

The next layer of stress is what does happen. All day, every day. Pupils' resistance to authority is expressed in all kinds of behaviours, and teachers have their individual *bêtes noires*. The one which twists my insides the most is the technique of non-response. A pupil is tearing small pieces of paper from an exercise book to make into pellets.

'James, stop doing that, please.'

James continues chatting to his neighbour as if nothing has been said. Surely he heard me? I approach, taking the chance that the incipient argument on the other side of the room will not erupt, and that the boy who needs instant reinforcement on the completion of each small task will be able to wait. James turns his back slightly more on me, continuing the conversation.

'Excuse me, James, I asked you to stop tearing the paper.'

There is neither the slightest movement of the head, nor the slightest hesitation in his voice. The discussion about who might be going to the match continues unimpeded. It's as if I'm not there.

So far, in this mini-incident, I have made a number of decisions. They relate to the priority to give to James, in comparison with the other interactions in the room which might require my attention — oh yes, bearing in mind the whole time the principle of positive reinforcement of behaviour, and the theoretical aim of my presence, which is to assist the learning process. They also relate to the appropriate demeanour and style of intervention, bearing in mind the certainty that non-intervention will result in the major disruption of pellets flying.

Now, however, is time for a larger decision. James has responded to me by totally ignoring me. What next? Retreat or escalation? This decision has to be taken while my head is pounding and my insides twisting from the provocation.

For me, for someone to pretend I just do not exist while I am speaking reasonably to him is almost unbearably stressful. The anger and the frustration boil up together, but the lid must be screwed down because the emotion is not permitted, because the response must be positive and professional.

It doesn't matter what I do next. If I decide the situation is such that a confrontation is inescapable, the adrenaline pumps, the heartbeat jumps, and here we go. But even if I retreat, to fight only some other battle which really counts, the damage is done. The educationists would mean, of course, the damage to the learning environment, and the damage poor teaching has done to James' life chances. But I mean, simply, the damage to me, to my professional self-esteem, to my stock of resilience, to my health and life expectancy. One more knock.

For teachers dealing with difficult classes, there are hundreds of negative interactions each day. Each one jolts. Each one must be dealt with without anger. Each one is exhausting, demoralising, and prevents us from teaching effectively. And each one is unavoidable. No-one can tolerate such a social environment, hour after hour, day after day, without damage to their long-term health. This is why teachers in such schools are drained, exhausted, and emotionally fragile by the end of the school day.

Yet some commentators appear to believe that such conditions are created by and acceptable to the victims. To suggest that teachers somehow willingly conspire in creating disorderly classrooms betrays a total ignorance of the experience of dealing with them. It is against all common sense. If commentators want more order in our classrooms, I can assure them that no-one wants that more than our teachers. And while the current focus is on the performance of teachers, we must all ask ourselves: are disorderly classrooms produced by the inadequate reactions of teachers, or by the unco-operative actions of the pupils? It is time to look again at our disorderly society for the explanation.

2

FAILING CITY

IT IS A COMMONPLACE THAT EDUCATION does not construct society, but reflects it. Teachers are well placed to view that reflection. In the inner city today, it is not a pretty sight. What seems to elude the rhetoricians, the theorists, and too many educationists, is that the ugliness brought to school each morning is not left at the gate.

There is a small group of middle class occupations whose function is to prevent the problems of those at the bottom of the social heap from spilling out and inconveniencing the rest of us. Social workers, of course, and local government officers in areas like housing, but also the criminal justice workers, many health workers — and, of course, teachers. I suppose that many other people can go their way with almost no connection with that other world. Unfortunately, they must pass beggars at an ever-increasing number of venues, and perhaps the kids hanging about at the local shopping centre, but otherwise they are in a different city.

Teachers in the kind of school I have described, and particularly primary teachers who have closer contact with the families, live closely with the other world. Teachers with pastoral responsibilities listen to accounts by pupils and their carers of lives which are quite different from their own. Teachers discover that poverty is a foreign country: they do things differently there. Not all teachers manage this; some secondary subject teachers are so exhausted by the effort of teaching the lessons and the hours of other useless work that they have neither the time, the energy, nor perhaps the kind of relationships with pupils, to listen to their stories.

Those of us who teach the children of the poor have struggled on through almost two decades in which poverty was off the agenda in Britain. While our stomachs were turned by the braces and BMW boom of the eighties, the poor were getting poorer. Quietly. Now, the Labour government establishes a social exclusion unit to co-ordinate anti-poverty policies. Is the debate on poverty to restart?

And what about a debate on class? The argument in this book is based on assumptions that social class remains a powerful concept to explain the social differentiation in our society, and that class culture is a powerful concept to explain the varied patterns of attitudes, beliefs and behaviour within our society. Class can only be defined meaningfully in terms of access to economic wealth. My concern is not with those who have a large degree of access, not least because they exclude themselves from the rigours of mass state education, but with those who have very little access.

Working class, or underclass?

Thirty years ago, it was assumed that the stratum of people furthest removed from wealth and power was the unskilled working class. As the label suggests, its members had no qualifications, and could obtain only unskilled work which was generally the lowest paid. It also tended to be the least secure, being casual, or temporary, or seasonal. For some, low paid work would be interspersed with periods of unemployment. A recent development had been the availability of work for married women, so that a family's luck might vary between having two earners and none. For others, secure employment produced a regular and reliable income. Another variable which had some effect was the state of the national economy; although the post-war period had seen steady growth, and virtually full employment, cyclical fluctuations produced variations in demand for unskilled labour.

Nevertheless, the state of the unskilled working class was that most people could expect to be in work some of the time, although their incomes did not allow them to be full participants in the growing culture of consumerism. Oh, what a golden age!

Well, not quite, because the unskilled working class was poor, relatively and sometimes absolutely. As compared with the population generally, these people had the lowest incomes, the worst accommodation, the largest families, the worst health and life expectancy, the least access to public services. Children of all ages frequently turned up for school hungry, dirty and ragged, and with no expectation that state education could improve their life chances.

Thirty years ago, however, changes were under way. One was the great acceleration in massive municipal schemes to demolish the slum housing in the inner cities, and the rehousing of whole neighbourhoods in huge new estates of tower blocks and houses, often on the edges of the cities. This amounted to a mass migration of the unskilled working class, and although the distance in miles was small, poor public transport links made it seem larger. To this day, these estates are isolated, geographically and socially.

Another change has been the decline of traditional industries, which in many cases provided employment for whole towns, including the unskilled working class. On top of that there have been various economic and technological changes which together have produced the growth of mass unemployment.

The difficulty in analysing this situation was increased by the government's attitude to unemployment statistics, since they have been defined and collected in a way designed to mystify rather than illuminate the question of how many people would like a job. Is the true figure under 2 million or over 4 million, or something in between? In fact, government figures for 1998 suggest the former for those unemployed on the International Labour Organisation definition, and the latter for those who have no job but would like one. The true figure must make a qualitative difference to our analysis of trends in class structure.

There is also some doubt now about the numbers of people in society's lowest stratum. There is the rumour about the huge growth in the English urban version of the disappeared ones — a trend exacerbated by the great poll tax fiasco — in which a substantial proportion of the population does not exist, as far as official statistics are concerned. It does not register to vote, does not have a settled abode. In many parts of our larger cities, this population is ever shifting. Such areas have always been a mecca for misfits. In addition, families migrate from Bolton and Bosnia. The flow of political refugees seems never-ending. Many of them join those ethnic minority groups for whom racism and physical insecurity are added to all the other insecurities.

The total effect of economic, social and political developments over the last thirty years has been a substantial worsening in the position of the poor relative to the population as a whole. The real income of the unskilled working class may have increased slightly, but very much less than other classes; in particular, there has been a substantial increase in the number of people able to indulge in conspicuous consumption. The employment situation has deteriorated significantly. Jobs are hard to find, and much more insecure. Low paid jobs have become relatively worse paid.

From the point of view of class analysis, the question is: do the changes of the past thirty years amount to a qualitative change in the relative access to economic wealth for an identifiable group? My answer, from the perspective of the classroom, is 'yes'. We are justified in using a new term to describe a new situation. The unskilled working class has become very much smaller, and the class *characterised by an expectation of unemployment* very much larger.

Of course, like all other sociological analysis, we are talking of tendencies. There were always elements within working class communities who never worked, but when they were the exception rather than the rule, their position could be explained in psychological terms ('the undeserving poor').

Now, we have a significant class of people whose relation to the economy is different from the class who might be called by some 'wage slaves'. This class is separated from the economy, in the sense that its normal condition is unemployment. Thirty years ago, in the most deprived areas of our cities, perhaps a third of men were out of work. But this meant that a majority of men were in work. Now, we can find areas where virtually no-one has a job, and where whole families have been without work for as long as they can remember. This represents a qualitative change. Where available, jobs are casual, temporary, and most work is within the informal economy. The wages are the lowest, in many cases lower in cash terms than they were ten years ago. At the same time, Social Security staff work under instruction to save public funds by avoiding informing applicants of their rights, and the unemployed, now laughingly renamed job-seekers, have to go through ever more convoluted hoops to qualify for benefits. So this new class is characterised by unemployment as normality, with income from work and benefits reduced in real terms.

I believe this class fits the Marxist concept of the lumpenproletariat. For Marx, it had to be defined as a class separate from the proletariat because its lack of permanent relationship to capital, in the form of employment, would prevent it from developing the class consciousness which would lead the proletariat to become a revolutionary force. The lumpenproletariat, then, was a thoroughly unreliable crowd, even though it performed the important service for capital of constituting a reserve army of labour. In the lower parts of the economic cycle, the existence of the unemployed helped to keep a downward pressure on wages; at the top of the cycle, production could be maximised by the temporary employment of at least some of its members.

What we have, as the century comes to an end, spread across the country, in the council estates and slums in the cities, in the vast estates sprawling round their edges, and in towns which have lost the industries which were their reason for being, is a new class, a class separated from the rest of society and the mainstream economy, a class which could be called the lumpenproletariat, but which is more generally known as *the underclass*. In this book, I use the term underclass. Some of those working against poverty object to the term because of its pejorative overtones. I do not use it here with any moral implications, but in a purely analytical way, and because I believe it is an apt term to describe social reality. In the modern western economy, there is a tremendous gap between the lumpenproletariat and all other classes, because the others have at least some access, however unequally, to economic wealth. Everyone else can play the consumption game to some extent. Hence, the utility of the euro-term, social exclusion, to describe this division.

It seems to me that the government wishes to use the terminology of exclusion, possibly to avoid mentioning that nasty word poverty, and certainly to avoid that old-Labour and outmoded interest in class. Obviously, there are categories other than the underclass who are excluded from society, such as those with problems of ageing, disability, and so on. But we delude ourselves if we do not understand that the problem of poverty and exclusion in our society is overwhelmingly a problem of the underclass.

An underclass culture

A class is defined by the relationship of its members to economic wealth, and to power. The relationship is shared, and so, therefore, is the general life experience. In its turn, this experience generates a culture — a class culture — by which I mean ways of behaving, sets of attitudes and beliefs, which are a response to the life experience, which are shared, and which are reproduced from generation to generation as long as the material circumstances remain. The concept of class culture, incidentally, explains why the description of its forms should not be interpreted as a moral lecture. A culture is a rational response to the circumstances of people's lives.

To give an extreme example, it could be argued that any reasonable young person, facing the awfulness and hopelessness of a future within the underclass, and with the history of an underclass upbringing, might conclude that it makes perfect sense to blot out that reality as often as possible by the use of narcotic substances. From the point of view of middle class teachers, we might say the sensible thing to do would be to use the education system to improve life chances. The crucial thing is, however, that such a sentiment has been produced by a completely different life experience. The teacher, with few exceptions, has not been there, or done that. The underclass youth has a particular point of view, a particular experience, and from that point of view the behaviour is rational. Of course, a culture gains its own strength, and elements of it, particularly ceremonial and artistic representations, may persist long after the material circumstances which produced it have disappeared.

I believe it is clear that the underclass has now sufficient size and persistence to have generated an identifiable culture. It may well share many characteristics with the culture of the unskilled working class, but there are vital differences. Its features derive from the state of unemployment which is the normal condition.

Technically, members of the underclass must be seeking work to qualify for Job-seekers Allowance. In reality, there is no expectation of or search for employment. Income is derived from 'ducking and diving' — petty crime, genuine or fiddled welfare benefits, the edges of the informal economy.

In a secular society, work is a strongly defining feature of people's lives, giving point to existence. For the underclass, existence tends to be pointless. The behavioural implication of this feature is what others would call inconsequential behaviour; there is no need to have regard to what might happen tomorrow as a result of what I do today — it does not matter. When a pupil says 'Who cares?' in response to a warning, teachers will often interpret that as bravado. When an underclass pupil says it, it often means the pupil really does not care.

Perhaps the major feature of the underclass culture is the sense of separation from society, resulting from the separation from the economy. The poor are among us but not of us. They view this relationship with resentment and antagonism. Institutions of the state are viewed with a particular suspicion. On the one hand the realities of power dictate that the state must be dealt with — money to be screwed out of the social, trouble with the law best avoided, school to be attended — but on the other hand, the state is out to get us.

At the same time, there seems to be little cohesion within the class, little sense that 'we're all in this together against the rest of the world', and suspicion of 'the other' may well extend to neighbours. Just as Marx predicted of the lumpenproletariat, there is little class consciousness. To put it another way, within the underclass there is a complete absence of the 'stakeholder' concept, to use yet another term recently invented (but apparently dropped just as quickly) to avoid the use of class analysis in political debate.

So inner city teachers, along with the other shock troops of the welfare state, are in a position to observe a way of life which is hidden from most people most of the time. What are its characteristics?

Above all, and everywhere, and in everything, is the anger. Children and adults of the underclass are defensive, aggressive, or both. They live on short fuses. So many public places are filled with tension. In London, the worst thing about a tube journey is not the fear that the escalators will catch fire again, nor the rush-hour squeeze as tight as any old-time football crowd; no, the worst thing is being with a large number of fellow humans, all of whom (except the tourists) are simultaneously trying to look at everyone else to assess the risk they pose, at the same time as trying to avoid catching anyone's eye in case it is considered provocative.

Another determining feature of the culture is the sheer misery of material existence. Let no-one forget that being poor means being hungry, being cold, having inadequate clothing, inadequate shelter. These days, the poor may refuse to be cold or inadequately clothed, but that just makes the struggle for resources more difficult. Being poor means a struggle to get by that must dominate every waking hour, unless it becomes so overwhelming that it must be blotted out.

This struggle gives rise, most dangerously, to a lack of self-esteem so fundamental that life is, indeed, cheap. This has implications for attitudes to
violence, dangerous behaviour, and the use of intoxicants. From the point of
view of the middle class reader, the lives of these people are solitary, nasty,
brutish — and short, as compared with European norms.

Children of the underclass form a significant proportion of the school population in the inner city, and on some estates on the edges of our cities. In what
condition, then, do children in such circumstances reach school each morning?
Some will show obvious signs of neglect; scruffy, unwashed clothes and
scruffy, unwashed bodies. In this country of such wealth that many people
spend large sums on buying water although it is available free from their taps,
how many people understand a secondary school which feels it has to
provide a bath to cater for pupils who turn up too dirty to be tolerated?

In a nation whose children grow larger with each generation, many of these
will be obviously smaller. For some years, I coached a rugby team at a school
serving an estate for the poor. We were annihilated every week. I am sure my
coaching was not very good, but a major factor was that every week the largest
boy in our team was smaller and lighter than almost anyone in the opposing
team. The only exception occurred when we played the other local school.

Not only smaller, children from the underclass are much less healthy than
others. The incidence of respiratory conditions seems to increase continuously amongst children generally, but amongst the underclass they seem
almost the norm rather than the exception. When such a pupil complains of
a headache or stomach ache severe enough to prevent participation in a
lesson, the judgement by the teacher as to whether the complaint is genuine
is made more difficult by the stronger likelihood that it is. They also seem to
suffer from more serious conditions more frequently.

Apart from their health, many underclass children will reach school in the
morning obviously tired, because they go to bed late, and are likely to have
interrupted nights. It is by no means uncommon for them to fall asleep in
class, with a tiredness which the teacher could defeat only by physically
shaking the child.

At secondary age, pupils' physical condition is complicated by the likelihood of the use of a variety of mind-altering substances. They are growing
up in close proximity to drink and drugs. They will know adults caught up in
the sub-cultures of their abuse, and understand their utility in blotting out
unendurable reality. This is just one more aspect of their culture into which
they are becoming socialised.

The most common such substance is alcohol. As adolescents, they understand the essential calculation of kick per pound, which produces a rating of

drinks according to their alcohol content and cost. This is not entirely new, of course; in my first year of teaching an eleven-year-old lad in my tutor group often missed Monday mornings with a hangover. Now, however, adolescents have access to alcohol independently of their parents, and I detect a more desperate determination to get smashed.

What is new is the general availability in the inner city of illegal drugs. There are complex patterns of drug use by young members of the underclass. Geographical and sub-cultural maps would be required to describe the phenomenon. In some places, the quick drag behind the bike shed at break has taken on a new dimension for smokers from all classes. Then, in some underclass communities, secondary aged pupils are involved in other kinds of substance abuse.

In my experience, pupils are rarely in school seriously under the influence of drink or drugs, because these are largely activities of the night, but many will be suffering the after effects the next morning. Headaches, memory loss, mood swings all create difficulties for the teacher, and add to the pupils' unwillingness to take part in learning.

The underclass and the family

However, it is not the physical but the emotional and social health which is the source of most concern. In the city generally, family structures have changed radically. Amongst the underclass, certainly, family structure is characterised by instability. I am certain that one of the major problems is that a permanently unemployed male is deprived of his breadwinner role, does not find the child care role congenial, and therefore has no place in the family. So many underclass households have a rapid turnover of men, family or partners of the central mother character.

Poverty breeds stress, and stress breeds unstable relationships, giving rise to complicated family structures; many women have a number of children each by different fathers. There may be frequent changes of arrangements for child care, with friends or extended family involved.

Women of the underclass often begin child rearing at a very young age; having rejected schooling and, by implication, the mainstream economy, motherhood is a role which seems to confirm adulthood and independence. Generation after generation, they learn the hard way that they have imprisoned themselves. Many young mothers, without any permanent or reliable support, and without the cushion of cash, find the role a struggle. Many children of the underclass change schools frequently, as they live with a succession of relatives.

Even in families with some stability, relationships are difficult. The cause is poverty. When life is dominated fortnight in, fortnight out, by the fact that there is no way the ends can meet, it is not surprising that tempers get frayed, people get emotionally exhausted and people look for ways out or for ways to forget. It is impossible to over-emphasise the effect of poverty on attitudes and behaviour. If a household finds itself poor, but is within an extended family or community where this is not the norm, it may hold a hope of recovering from it. There may be emotional or practical support from the community.

I belong to a sports club. There is a general understanding that when we're at the bar, an unemployed member should not stand their round. Not only are the rest of us in work, but everyone expects the unlucky person to get a job fairly soon. If the unemployment or other cause of poverty is short-lived, the assets built up in better times may help to see the household through.

In underclass communities, things are different. In the first place, the material struggle is permanent, and there is no asset-base to support people in hard times. In the second place, everyone else is in the same boat. There is no-one who can give material support, and there is no local model of comfort or prosperity as an aspiration. If you have not been able to work for a long time, or perhaps ever, and most people you know are in the same situation, what hope or expectation can you have that things will ever improve? It is the length and depth of poverty which creates its distinctive culture, the culture of the underclass.

Them and us

Such experience produces an over-arching negative attitude to the world. It is compounded by the constant bombardment of images of wealth and inducements to consume. Out there, in the shopping centre, is a world from which the underclass is excluded. On top of that, in the cities, is the further feeling of exclusion arising from having a skin colour different from the one which dominates the outside world.

Members of the underclass perhaps cannot explain the forces which produce their social position, so the negativity, the anger, the resentment is directed at 'them'. 'Them' might take many forms, because it includes most of society. Crime is justified because its victims are 'them', and 'they' can afford it. Unfortunately, of course, in practice the easiest targets for crime are people closest to the criminals both geographically and socially.

'They' are most clearly visible as authority. People in authority are guarding the wealth and privilege of society, directly keeping out the underclass. Never mind that the bus driver is, these privatised days, a low paid and exploited worker, she (increasingly) has a uniform, asserts rules against the rowdy, and demands high fares for short journeys. All those who seem to be maintaining the apparatuses of a hostile state may be regarded as 'them'. There may be a continuum of contempt, but the police, social workers, the staff at the housing and benefit offices, and yes, teachers are all the objects of suspicion or outright opposition.

Many children come from families where hostile, negative emotions are universal, and are themselves hostile and negative in all their relationships. All are imbued with this 'them and us' perspective, which at the very least makes all agencies of the state 'them', and for some, to whom life really does seem like the war of all against all, makes all strangers 'them'. Many of these children, then, are unable to make any trusting or stable relationships even with their peers. Their friendships are uneasy, temporary, and built on some superficial transient advantage to be gained by the relationship. They are quick to take offence, and quick to give it, and respond to offence with a rapid escalation to verbal and physical aggression.

They are alienated from school from the beginning. School attempts to impose an order which they do not experience outside and do not accept. The school's staff are agents of an authority they reject, just as they reject, of course, all figures of authority in the society from which they are separated. As we have seen, it is not so much that many pupils disobey their teachers; it is more that they seem oblivious to instructions, that they do not accept the nature of the relationship of teacher and pupil as defined by the school and dominant forces within society.

I am not saying that a five-year-old, or a fifteen-year-old, from the underclass, if asked about their attitudes to school, will say something like 'I reject schooling as an apparatus of control imposed by a hostile state which is determined to maintain but repress a reserve army of labour.' What I am saying is that they do not have the theory or the vocabulary, but that their lives in school make that statement.

Hence a struggle.

Failing city

Our cities, including the massive council estates around their edges, are characterised by this struggle, an uneasy co-existence between groups of people with deep mutual antagonisms. The underclass develops its culture precisely because of its relationships to other classes, which live in close proximity. The extremes of poverty and wealth found in our society can be visited within a short walk. Our society now is one of the most economically unequal in the developed world.

My view is that these characteristics have created *an environment which fails*.

Our cities fail to provide the quality of life which our wealth as a society should be able to create for all. While the wealthy cruise in their insulated limousines, frustrated at the traffic jams and nervous about theft or damage, the poor suffer more frustration at the increasingly failing public transport system. While the wealthy occupy mansions costing far more than the average lifetime wage, worried about break-ins and muggings, the poor endure damp, cold, and overcrowding. While the wealthy consume the 'good things' in life without end, and without needing to count the cost, the poor see the objects of consumption, and the inducements to consume, from the outside.

Some describe our cities in quite another way. They are lively, innovative, exciting. The young seek the entertainment. But I wonder whether, as the young things make their way down the Strand after a bright and expensive evening in Covent Garden, the numerous blanketed bodies in doorways cast any sort of shadow over their fun.

To speak like this is not the politics of envy. It is the politics of a sense of fundamental unfairness. Our cities are failing because they encapsulate and support the unfairness of our society which impoverishes all, the wealthy and the poor and the millions in between. Frustrations and insecurities damage the lives of all of us who live in the city.

All the institutions in our cities struggle, in their different ways, with this failure. For some, the struggle is to work round it. For others, the struggle is to cope with it. And for a few, the struggle is to eradicate it. Financial institutions refuse to deal with people from the wrong postcode. Bus companies withdraw from routes which come under attack too frequently. But schools, amongst others, stand within the struggle and become part of it.

Schools for the underclass are one site where these social antagonisms are played out. They are described as failing, but the real failure is in the social arrangements revealed so starkly in our cities.

This is not a book with a historical perspective, because my argument is about how things are now, and what can be done about it. We know, not least from oral history, that alienation from state education is not a new phenomenon; it is as old as state education itself. However, the form of struggle arising from that alienation has changed significantly in recent years.

For one thing, those in authority are now precluded from the use of brute force to assert it. The struggle for order in inner city schools depends on a myriad of inter-relating factors, some of which are discussed within this book. However, an important consideration here is the simple numbers game. Schools which are comprehensive, in which there is a social mix, are dealing with a minority of the alienated underclass. They can use a variety of tactics.

Using more compliant pupils as role models, such schools can incorporate some of them, and manage the rest, albeit with difficulty.

But what of the schools which are populated largely by the underclass? There, it is not an overstatement to describe the situation as the staff vs. the rest. Teachers can hope for no allies when faced with disobedience in the classroom, no others to support the call for a work ethic.

In the debate on quality of schooling, we must not forget all this. But it is being forgotten. We shall not improve life chances for all in our society until we remember the society from which young people arrive in our schools. It is a society, in our inner cities, imbued with poverty, need, anguish, alienation, fear, and rejection. Let us start from there.

3

THE SCHOOL IN THE CITY

I HAVE DEFINED THE UNDERCLASS SCHOOL as one whose intake consistently contains a proportion of children of underclass origins sufficient to become the strongest single determinant of its life. Some readers might be doubting that this categorisation of schools by social class of intake is valid. Excluding those few areas which continue with 11+ selection, we have comprehensive secondary schools. In the cities, school admissions policies allowing for parental choice are combined with a large number of schools within travelling distance. Surely this means that comprehensive schools take pupils from a range of backgrounds?

The picture is a lot more complicated than that. It is true that the populations of England's cities remain socially mixed. Indeed, some of the urban regeneration programmes of recent years have increased the proximity of rich and poor, middle classes, working classes, and underclass. The populations of city schools, then, in total, are socially mixed. In order to understand how we come to have schools for the underclass, we must examine the complex ranking system applied to secondary schools in the city.

The hierarchy of status

There is a finely graded hierarchy of secondary schools within cities. Just as the form of the class structure changes with developments in occupational structure, so the school hierarchy changes with administrative arrangements. Just as individuals move within the class structure, so do schools move up and down the hierarchy. It is not the purpose of this book to analyse in detail the fine gradations, but a flavour can be conveyed by using inner London as an example.

Until recently, inner London schools were administered by a single authority which had a long-standing egalitarian approach. Sophisticated procedures were in force to try to ensure a balanced intake to its secondary schools, which all declared themselves to be comprehensive. Substantial financial and professional support resources were allocated to schools according to perceived need. Did the unceasing best efforts of the Inner London Education

Authority (ILEA) to create equality of esteem have the desired effect? In truth, some schools obstinately persisted in being more equal than others.

The hierarchy I refer to is the one created by parental perception. Let us not go into the intricate web of conversations about the style of uniform, or lack of it, the behaviour on the buses, 'I hear that headmaster don't stand no nonsense,' and such and such which did and does create and recreate school reputations and images; that forever changing ladder of local evaluations of schools. Let us not check the degree of agreement between such perception and the present realities of the schools being discussed; let us not, for the moment, ask ourselves how far the parents' charter has impinged on this process, or what is made of the information on exam results.

In each part of the city, there is an agreed rating of secondary schools, recreated each autumn as parents of top juniors begin the painful process of placing their offspring. I don't suggest that there is anything like 100% correspondence in parental rating; for one thing, there are class and ethnic biases. Nor can the hierarchy be measured simply by the number of parents choosing particular schools; between the processes of rating and formal choice, there is a mediation in which the primary school plays a vital role. 'St.Ethel's is terribly oversubscribed, you know — perhaps your Jane would prefer the P.E. facilities at the Ken Livingstone School.'

At the top of the heap are the schools which more or less reluctantly gave up their official grammar school status when the ILEA abolished secondary selection by the 11+ exam in the seventies. Almost all were small, voluntary aided schools supported by the churches or by charitable foundations with church influences. Is it surprising that institutions, around which there had been elaborate mechanisms to exclude 80% of London's children for nearly a century, should persistently be regarded as desirable? As grammar schools, they shared the characteristics of those described by the pioneers of British sociology of education all those years ago.

Overwhelmingly and unashamedly middle class institutions, they each trawled large segments of the capital for those certificated by the 11+ as the cream of the available academic talent. (Readers need not be detained here by the oh-so-delicate hierarchy within this group of schools, so carefully explained to top junior parents each year as the results came out.) The few hailing from working class homes were expected to learn the ropes as soon as possible. Curiously, many of these schools were situated in far from middle class locations, but they recognised no commitment to their locality; their open allegiance was to the middle class of a whole quarter of the city.

A few, when 'invited' to move to a balanced intake procedure, could not bite the bullet, and became independent. Most, however, must have guessed that their place in the common consciousness of London parents would guarantee that, while a certain amount of bending might be required while the wind blew strong, their position in the hierarchy could be retained. And so it was that, right up until the abolition of the ILEA in 1990, and the coincident introduction of a whole new set of methods of categorising and evaluating schools, by a number of strategies on the part of the schools, and by social factors such as the persistence of perceptions about them (a beautiful example of the self-fulfilling prophecy, this), these schools remained at the top of the heap, second only to private schools.

And beneath, so to speak, the ex-grammar schools? Let us examine just two types of schools.

There are the 'successful comprehensives'. Many of them established in buildings new in the fifties and sixties, with their own playing fields and the best of facilities, these schools were typically placed towards the outer edges of the ILEA area. More importantly, many of these new schools attracted, sooner or later, a balanced intake. The conventional use of that term is that on entry, pupils exhibited a spread of attainment roughly in line with that for London's eleven-year-olds as a whole. Another way it might be put is that the class backgrounds of the intake reflected the class mix of the city. The ability of such schools to struggle up the hierarchy was based on their ability to convert the more able end of their intakes into academic successes. Many also were of the size to be able to offer a wider range of curricular and extra-curricular choices than their grammar school competitors, and could appear vibrant, confident, modern. The intellectual bourgeoisie, finding they could have their cake, a 'comprehensive', and eat it, a confidence that their child would obtain the university place and the music tuition and the place in the rugby team, primed the helix of achievement and popularity which is self-perpetuating.

And then, there are the schools which were once called 'sinks'. Often, they are located in the most deprived areas of the city. They are in old buildings which once were unpopular elementary schools, then became unpopular secondary modern schools, and finally comprehensive schools in name. The salient point, the defining point, the overwhelmingly determining point, and the point which is always ignored by the successful schools movement, is the massive social uniformity of the intake. The casual observer, noting the multitudes of ethnicities represented in such schools, might find this description strange; but for our purposes, the vital factor is that the families of these schools' pupils have migrated from all over the world and become members of the same social class — the European urban underclass.

These schools are at risk in a number of ways. They are always at risk of failing to attract sufficient pupils to be viable; until recently, of course, this meant viable in an educational sense, but now it means in a financial sense. They are at risk in terms of the social stability and peace of the school community. And now, they are officially 'at risk' — the phrase used by the Office for Standards in Education to denote a school likely to fail to deliver a satisfactory education. One of the questions to be asked later is, how is it that the worst schools in the country happen to be the ones with the most deprived intakes? The history of Ofsted inspections seems to suggest that such is the case.

This division of secondary schools in inner London into four types, the private, the ex-grammar, the successful comp, and the sink, is of course an outline sketch. They are pure types, and reality is seldom that simple. There are other sets, and subsets; they all merge imperceptibly. In particular, there is a large group of schools, placed in the hierarchy between the successful comprehensive and the sink, which might well be categorised as 'ordinary'.

However, this hierarchy has a strong persistence over the years. Individual schools may change their rating, but this is likely to be over a long period, and unlikely to involve a radical change in position on the ladder.

I have described a London hierarchy, but similar maps could be drawn of our other cities. In each of them, by a complex system of grading and choice, we have a small number of secondary schools in which the young of the underclass are the majority group, the culture of the underclass defines the pupils' values and behaviour, and where teachers and learning are opposed or marginalised. There are also underclass schools on estates in and around major towns, where the community is monocultural and the school serves the community.

New labels, old status

And where, it might be asked, do the administrative reforms of the nineties fit in all this? What of the vanguard of the individualist meritocracy, the grant-maintained movement? Did opting out either improve a school, or improve perceptions of it in the community? What it did was to confer the same label of exclusivity which otherwise has been achieved by being voluntary aided, or perhaps being grammar. However, a large proportion of opting out schools were just those which already benefited from such a label — or, as some would say, they always had ideas above their station. For the most part, then, GM status has only confirmed the local hierarchy, rather than altering its balance. In addition, there are other categories established explicitly in order to increase 'variety and choice'.

The City Technology Colleges have managed to avoid the spotlight, but they are the object of even more inequitable treatment than the GM schools, continuing to receive sums of money direct from the government that every other secondary school in the country would envy. When that scheme failed to attract private sponsors, the government turned to the Technology School ploy, which was a mixture of private and government money on a more limited basis, again for a chosen few. These initiatives together have a reinforcing effect on parental perceptions of hierarchy, and increase the polarisation of schools.

Of course, any new government looking to equity was bound to abolish the market ideology driven variety of funding and governance, or so we thought. As has often been pointed out, the 1944 Education Act incorporated an historic compromise between church and state on the funding and control of schools, a compromise which was endangered by the grant-maintained movement. It would be necessary for any new government to restore it by returning schools which had opted out back to where they had come from, be it local authority or voluntary aided status, and to abolish those other gimmicks which involved unfair funding and status.

The Labour Party's opposition to opting out was as reasonable when it was introduced as it is now. The refusal of the Labour government to remove this status hierarchy is an action which defines it as a short-termist populist government quite without principle. It is astonishing for the government to allocate such massive amounts of public funds to bodies which are elected only by themselves, and will continue to behave with only limited reference to the system of which they are supposed to be a part. The continued existence of foundation schools will merely permit the persistence of artificial gradations of status which encourage the further polarisation of intakes and performance. It will be a serious impediment to the government's drive towards higher standards for all.

Schools choose parents

The place of individual schools within the hierarchy is very largely agreed within communities. However, this does not make individual schools equally attractive to the various communities. Take Dulwich College, which being a day school is part of the south London hierarchy. Whilst across the city, parents of a certain kind anxiously assess their bank balances and the chances of their son passing the entrance exam, parents of another kind in Southwark would refuse a place if offered. The same process works, in subtly different ways, throughout the hierarchy of schools, until we reach the bottom. Even there, we find certain kinds of parent who positively choose such schools, who support the school in the usual ways, and who form action groups to oppose proposals for closure.

So we have a system of choice, in which parents from different classes use different criteria. Incidentally, teachers dealing with admissions say what research has suggested: that few parents are interested in the league tables of exam performance at Key Stages 3 and 4. They seem to understand that output is determined largely by intake. No, they are more keen to discover whether discipline is good, whether their child will be happy at the school, what facilities and subject choices will be available. Then their choices are influenced by the primary school head's advice.

The various components of the 1988 Education Reform Act, taken together, and substantially unchanged by the 1998 legislation, make the hierarchy all-important for secondary schools. Those at the top have become relatively more popular, and those at the bottom relatively more unpopular. Before the reforms allegedly aimed at improving parental choice, over 9 out of 10 parents were able to enrol their children at the secondary school of their choice. Most recent figures show that the proportion has dropped to 8 out of 10.

What are the results of this process for the social mix within secondary schools? The most popular schools are oversubscribed several times over. The result is, by definition, a selection process, carried out by the school, or by the local authority. The schools which are most oversubscribed may operate an unofficial policy of social selection, in one of two directions. Some seek the most advantageous intake, that is the most middle class. Others will hope for an intake mixed roughly in the proportions of the population in the area. The schools which are undersubscribed operate only one policy — bums on seats. All applicants welcome. In short, the current details of the 11+ transfer process are relatively unimportant. The results of the process remain comparatively stable across generations. The typology of schools I described earlier is reproduced year by year.

Location? It's no clue to intake

This book is about those at the bottom of the heap. All schools have pupils whose attitude and behaviour places a great strain on the institution. The question is, what is the social mix? What are the numbers, what are the proportions? What kind of pupil is in the ascendancy, what class values set the tone? Some of London's former grammar schools are as comfortable places to work in as any secondary schools in the country.

Not so long ago, I visited one, a girls school, to give a talk. This school is proud to be comprehensive, scrupulously observes the letter and spirit of the education authority's transfer procedures, and expects a mixed intake. The corridors were quiet and orderly, the pupils strangely (to me) deferential and polite. The pupils I addressed were that charming mixture of shy and alert. One in particular impressed me with her oral skills. 'Oh yes,' said the teacher afterwards, 'she's the daughter of...', and named a local MP.

The parents and pupils associated with the nearest neighbour school would be inclined to spit on him or his daughter in the unlikely event of coming across them. For although they are separated by a short walk, they are also separated by a social chasm which has only widened in the last twenty years. In this school, in which I have worked, the corridors are not quiet or orderly, and the pupils are not polite and certainly not deferential. In this school, there is no social mix. It is socially homogenous. It is a school for the underclass.

The two schools are much less than a mile apart. They are at opposite ends of the authority's league tables. This example illustrates the persistence of the patterns I describe through a variety of administrative changes in local government and education policy.

I myself attended grammar school in the same area in the late fifties and early sixties; the boys from our school were routinely abused and harassed by the boys from the 'rough' school. Since then, the rough school has been re-organised and re-named (twice), seen a variety of headteachers and styles of leadership — and has retained its identity and status throughout.

Similarly, the girls' school, then a grammar school of mystery and allure to us as sixth-formers, was known as a posh place. Naturally, this school has been careful to keep its name, but the transition from grammar to comprehensive some twenty years ago has left it virtually untouched. The example casts light on the proposition, voiced widely, that school failure must be the fault of the school because 'schools serving similar areas often perform very differently', to quote one official document.

Unfortunately, I have never heard either an education quango apparatchnik or a politician actually give an example. The problem with such an approach is that it makes mistaken assumptions about catchment areas, and about the cultural map of the city.

Travelling to school, the typical secondary pupil passes a number of other schools. Some schools attract pupils from a wide and scattered area; it is not unusual for a Year 7 intake to arrive from twenty, thirty, or even forty different primary schools. Even those schools which more consciously attempt to serve a particular community or area will also take many pupils from outside it. A map of home to school movement has no apparent pattern or tidiness: it is a myriad of criss-crossing paths.

Another factor is the close proximity in the city of areas of wealth and squalor, of mansions and hard-to-let council blocks. So the location of a school gives little necessary clue as to the addresses of its pupils, or their social backgrounds. If the official view actually is intended to mean that schools with similar intakes often perform very differently, the performance of geographically close schools is no evidence at all.

The school or the intake?

Am I denying that part of the differences in the performance is due to school related factors? Of course not. That would be ridiculous. Teachers welcomed the trend towards research which identifies factors within schools affecting levels of attainment. Teachers need to know, in the title of one of the early and most stimulating books on the subject, that 'school matters'. It would be hard for teachers in difficult schools to keep going without holding on to a belief that all this pain is worth something in the end. There is no point in being there unless we make a difference.

Of course, some schools are better than others at realising the potential, of creating good conditions for learning. Actually, as the research into 'value-added' shows, things are not as simple as that. The evidence from reputable academic study is that some schools seem to do better with some kinds of pupil, or with some prior attainment base, than other schools.

The trouble is that it has suited some, particularly politicians, in recent years to pretend that *only* school matters. Indeed, it would be difficult to justify simple league tables of exam performance without an assumption that, in some sense, all schools started with the same potential for achievement. The whole rhetoric of the government, both Tory and Labour, of Ofsted, of the popular media, depends on this. Those endless columns of SATs and GCSE scores might be reported in terms of the schools and authorities with the 'highest and lowest' results, but easily slip into 'best and worst performers'. 'How good is a secondary school?' Answer: 'What is the percentage of pupils gaining at least 5 GCSEs at grades A-C?'

Some of the people who talk like this are also supporters of selective education, and seem to think that grammar schools are proved to be good schools when they attain high grades, disregarding the fact that the pupils have been selected on the precise criterion that high grades are what they are predicted to achieve! The offence against logic is breathtaking.

The state we have reached is illustrated by the following. Recently, the educational statistician for the London Borough of Hackney showed that there is an uncanny inverse correlation between the rank order of local education authorities in success on this criterion and the number of pupils entitled to free school meals. My point is not that this is useful evidence, but my astonishment that this repetition of sixties research was newsworthy.

It might be said that the simplistic equation of high grades with good school is a fault of our media. Not so. This book is about the low achieving schools, the 'bad schools'. No less a postholder than Her Majesty's Chief Inspector of Schools has used an identical asocial rhetoric which simply blamed, at first, bad teaching, and, increasingly, bad management for the schools labelled bad.

What is needed is the restoration of some balance in the debate about school performance. What is needed is to take into account not only our knowledge of school effects, but also the seemingly discarded knowledge about external determinants of performance. This would include a more realistic acceptance of the comparative weightings of these two types of factors.

Teachers assume that what they often call the home background is by far the largest determinant of success. A 1997 paper from the DfEE, on the value added between GCSE and A level across the country, found that 'on average, some 90 per cent of the variation in value added is between individuals within institution and cohort, with 8 per cent between institutions.' To understand the success of the posh school, then, and the failure of the sink school, we need to understand the kind of people who attend them.

Do they look smart?

The classroom behaviour described in Chapter 1 is typical of the sink school. What are its other features? What distinguishes it from schools with mixed intakes? Let us examine the question through the issue of pupil dress.

What young people wish to wear is mediated through class and ethnic cultures, and through youth cultures. All of these inter-relate in complex and quickly changing ways, a process accelerated if not produced by consumerist forces. Many items, originally the property of one group, become universal. The Afro-Caribbean underclass boys' culture is particularly dominant, from a style point of view.

The trainer, for example, is a powerful item, and a frightening one for parents looking at price tags. Intrinsic to much underclass black youth culture is the aggressive assertion of capacity to consume. Thus it is important to wear not just the right brand, but the right model, which is the newest and most expensive. Manufacturers have responded with the alacrity predicted by theorists of capitalism, by inventing frequent 'advances' in design. Since each advance amounts almost to a requirement, teenagers will do what they must to acquire the trainer. It is now common for young people to be set upon by gangs, not for their money or their bikes, but for their trainers and other labelled garments. Of course, this cultural item spreads out across the ethnicities and classes, and ripples into arguments between the white middle class eight-year-old and his mother about the brand of trainer she will buy.

There is much more that could be written about particular garments, and dress style in general. For my purpose, it is necessary only to note that such issues are important for underclass youth. They are important for the youth of other classes as well, but mixed in with other, sometimes conflicting values. How does this impinge on what pupils wear to school?

There are few secondary schools which do not insist on uniform. Although a very British custom, school uniform is very widely supported by parents. That is not to say that uniform is not a bone of contention between pupils and teachers. The battle is unending on shirts buttoned up and tucked in, ties, skirt length, sensible shoes (not trainers), and so on.

In many schools, however, the battle is ritualistic. The pupils accept the right of schools to order their affairs, accept, with more or less reluctance, the right of schools on uniform, and push against the boundaries only as much as they would do on any issue of authority. In any tutor group, there will be just a few who persistently try it on — and with a bit of extra persistence, the teacher can persuade the rebel to fall into line, not only with the school rules, but with the mass of other pupils.

Most teachers are happy to play this game on the basis that they would rather be holding the line on something ultimately trivial than on some essential part of pupil compliance. These days, they also have the feeling that the appearance of their pupils while on the street might have a bearing on the school's market position; research suggests they are right.

Schools for the underclass also have uniform. Getting pupils to wear it is a different order of task. Since neither pupils nor parents accept the legitimacy of the school to direct them, and since appearance occupies a particularly important place in their youth culture, parents generally support children in non-compliance. As in all aspects of behaviour, it is the sheer scale of the refusal which makes the imposition of uniform standards so difficult. Whereas most pupils will turn up on day one in Year 7 in a uniform provided by clothing grant, it does not take long for them to find their feet, compare notes, and start the slide away from compliance.

As they get older, perhaps a dozen of them will confront their tutor daily. The only way to wage the battle is on an individual basis. That suggests a dozen conversations on the lines of:

'Where's your blazer/tie/shoes?'

'At the cleaners/menders/my brother took mine/I left it at my gran's.'

'Have you brought a note explaining this?'

'I forgot/I asked my mum but she forgot/my mum wasn't in/I wasn't at home last night.'

'Right, I want you in your blazer/tie/shoes tomorrow.'

'I can't, because…'

'I'll give you a note for today, but I'll expect full uniform tomorrow.'

How many minutes is required for a dozen such conversations, and the associated notes? And is it more important for the tutor to confront the pupil on uniform, or on the absence last week for which there has still been no note? Or the fact that this is the third lateness this week? Of course, the conversation sets in train further time consuming follow-up the next day. The alternative strategy is the collective approach:

'Far too many of you are not in correct uniform. I expect you all to put that right by tomorrow.'

Old hands will not add, 'or else', because that would commit them to a course of time-consuming and probably unenforceable sanctions. (Why unenforceable? That is explained in Chapter 6.)

Another reason why it is more difficult to impose uniform standards in the school for the underclass is that pupils are less inclined than elsewhere to do as they are told, when they are told. As we saw earlier, this radically affects the shape of lessons. It also means that the pupil is less likely to appear the following day in correct uniform. The pupil who had no shoes might have them today, trainers in bag ready for later, but today no blazer and shirt untucked. In most schools, the battle will be won, only to be replayed next year with the next cohort. In the school for the underclass, the battle is continuous with every cohort.

The uniform question is a typical example of an aspect of school life which is routine is most schools, but problematic in schools for the underclass. The solidarity of the pupils in withholding consent undermines everything teachers try to do. Other aspects are attendance and punctuality.

Readers may ask, if these kids reject schooling, how come they turn up day by day? A good question. The first answer is, although underclass families may not respect the law, they respect its force. They recognise that the judicial system has some ability to make unpleasant things happen. It is true that sanctions against non-attendance are a mere pin-prick, in the form of letters, visits from busybodies, and threats. Some local authorities have got tough lately, and persuaded courts to demand large fines in the occasional case, so there is just the chance that the threat will amount to something. So it is worth doing just enough to keep the busybodies away.

The second answer is, where else would the kids go all day? School is a convenient, warm, dry place to meet your mates. You can have a laugh, plan your day, deal a bit (when older), and it can often provide an alibi when you have been the other side of the law while truanting.

On the other hand, there are definite drawbacks to attending school. You have to get up so early, or go through all the hassles of being late. You're being told what to do every minute of the day — some teachers just won't leave you alone. If you're not careful, they can make you look stupid by showing up what you can't do — like reading. To coin a phrase, teachers really jar you.

The outcome of all those balancing forces is that pupils from the underclass attend, but far less regularly than other children, and with far worse punctuality. From the teacher's perspective, this makes things more difficult in a number of ways. Firstly, as described above, absence and unpunctuality must be dealt with. Secondly, they make it more difficult to maintain pressure on other issues that are being raised, in terms of control and pastoral care. Thirdly, it is just one more impediment to any learning process, because, for so many pupils, there is no continuity.

But let me be candid: many teachers welcome the absence of some pupils, not just in staffroom banter but in their hearts, because their presence is so stressful, and so unlikely to lead to any educational success. They would not be human to think otherwise.

The path to failure

The government says it will have zero tolerance of failure. I think this means that it expects teachers to have zero tolerance of failure from their pupils. The constant presence of failure, of defeat, of exclusion, is a moral, philosophical and perhaps political problem, as well of course as a professional problem, for teachers of the underclass. In their more reflective moments, that is. The position of these young people is, indeed, intolerable: but, as I hope this book shows, it is beyond the power of their teachers to alter it. These young people are, overwhelmingly, educational failures, thus inexorably reproducing their class position. How does this happen?

To start at the beginning: underclass children enter primary school already far behind their contemporaries. This long-recognised reality is behind early years policies which allocate nursery education and day care provision according to social priority. The fact is, however, that whether three-year-olds receive 2 hours, 5 hours, or even 8 hours a day of professional care, it leaves between 16 and 22 hours each day of care by others.

Nursery education works, of course, but it cannot eliminate the comparative deficiency in learning readiness. Underclass five-year-olds are not very good at talking. They have a smaller vocabulary, and are less likely to speak in sentences. More generally, they are poor at conversation; that is, at the interaction which involves listening to another, and responding appropriately. This is connected with a general lack of social skills, the ability to relate to both peers and adults. Most children of this age are working through their infant egocentricity, but this is delayed in children of the underclass. Neither are they very good at playing. The lack of social skills means that they cannot play co-operatively with their peers, and when playing alone do not show the same imagination as other children. Infant teachers report a general worsening in the ability of five-year-olds to play, but it remains particularly pronounced in children of the underclass.

I am not going to attempt to describe the features of the lifestyle of the underclass which produce this comparative deficiency. Primary teachers gain insights from their relationships with carers, but it is for others to map the culture. Every teacher is aware, however, of the great instability of relationships for such children. I have hesitated to mention families, because I am not sure how much nuclear families exist. There is often a frequently changing set of carers, who may be from the extended family or not, and not even the mother is necessarily a constant figure. There may be also frequently changing accommodation, in which case the concept of home, as understood in other classes, cannot be applied.

In many primary schools in the city, as elsewhere, reception teachers find most of their pupils practised in looking at books, discussing what they see with adults and other children, and recognising some at least of the letters of the alphabet. They have started the journey to becoming readers. Children of the underclass, whose parents are themselves poor readers, are scarcely aware there is a journey to be undertaken. Some two years later, these tots, and their teachers, are judged on their ability to cope with nationally standard reading tasks. The results are obvious. Is the government seriously suggesting that by intoning 'zero tolerance of failure' at regular intervals, this phenomenon, which of course is as old as universal education, is to be eradicated?

Teachers welcome any new scheme which might help. There are many, most of which have useful features. Interventions with mothers soon after birth; involving mothers in early years provision; various literacy schemes for primary pupils, such as reading recovery; the National Literacy Strategy; they all make a difference. Recent research suggests that, through all the changes in fashions in teaching reading, through all the projects and supports, it seems as though average standards of reading competence have changed little over the years. Let's be realistic: children of the underclass, coping with lives of chaos and pain, are up against it when asked to learn the basic skills in primary schools, and teachers should not be blamed when they do not succeed in overcoming the odds. It certainly is not for want of trying.

As the primary years go on, underclass children fall further behind. It is not long before they realise their situation, and develop ways of dealing with their apparent failure. At the same time, they are becoming increasingly aware of the antagonism of those around them to schooling, and to the state and authority generally. As ever, primary schools and teachers are encouraged to consider negative behaviour within a model of individual pathology.

The Special Educational Needs Code of Practice, introduced in 1993, has reinforced this view. In order to obtain extra resources, such as guidance from other professionals, or an extra adult in the classroom, teachers must declare such pupils to be suffering emotional and behavioural difficulties. This does not work perfectly; in more difficult primary classes, almost all the pupils might be put on the SEN register for one reason or another, but that is administratively unmanageable, and the class teacher will select the most needy dozen or so. The government is to review the Code of Practice, largely because the costs of additional provision are literally out of the control of the education authority, but the fact that few pupils are removed from the SEN register, despite annual review, suggests that this scheme produces improvements as marginal as all the others.

And so to secondary school. The sorting process I have described produces secondary schools with a variety of social mixture in their intakes. To reiterate: by no means all pupils from the underclass attend schools for the underclass. In most London comprehensive schools, there will be anything from a smattering to a substantial group of them. There, simply because they are in a minority, their attitudes and behaviour can be challenged. They can be contained. As in primary schools, a difference can be made to their attainments and prospects; but it is a marginal difference.

However, there are a few schools where the large bulk of the intake is from the underclass. A large proportion of underclass children entering secondary school, aged 11, have reading ages of 7 or 8. For example, in one school described here, 50% of the intake has a reading age of less than 8. That is to say, they recognise comparatively few words, have poor phonic sense, can manage only simple texts, and thus need sustained individual tuition. If it was only a technical question, it would not be insurmountable, although there are resource issues. It is not. On top of this, by now, are psychological and cultural layers which make these pupils resistant to learning, and resistant to order within the school. That is what makes the task insurmountable.

Primary schools often expect, privately, some of the pupils they transfer to fail to integrate into their secondary schools. We have contained them, with increasing difficulty, and we did not take radical action because they will be leaving us. It is up to you in the secondary school to decide how to deal with them — but we expect you will have to transfer or exclude.

They are not wrong. A few of these eleven-year-olds have severe adjustment or mental health problems. Their behaviour is a source of diversion for the rest, and discomfort for the teacher, but in most secondary schools rapid action is taken to secure a more appropriate placement for such damaged people. However, this might take between two and six terms, and a pattern of disorderly behaviour is established in their classes.

Of course, this does not indicate that disorder is a matter of individual pathology. Experienced teachers are well aware that the removal of the most prominently difficult pupils from a class leads to the self-promotion of others to take over the role. The precise dynamics of the class might change, but where the majority tendency is oppositional, the result is always a few star-ring roles in disorder with a full supporting cast.

By definition, this is the position which secondary schools for the under-class find themselves in. The transfer process has concentrated into a few schools a majority of young people of the same kind. Their lives remain as chaotic and painful as ever, but with longer personal histories, including, crucially, a history of failure at school, and a greater awareness of the alien-ation from social institutions felt by their elders.

On top of that, it is not long before they have to cope with adolescence, and that search for identity which appears to be becoming more difficult for young people from all classes. What identity is there for those whose community is, objectively, excluded from society, and whose own exclusion is becoming more and more established with each day of growing up? No wonder they join their elders in seeing school as just another repressive institution, like the law, the council, and the 'social'.

So, as they progress (no, that is not quite the right word) through secondary school, young people of the underclass have a growing sense of separation from it. Their willingness to learn decreases. The gap between their attain-ments and those of young people in general continues to grow. In Year 11, fewer than 10% of them will achieve 5 GCSEs at grades A-C. Many simply won't bother turning up for the exams, or will attend if a teacher turns up on their doorstep on the morning of the exam and cajoles them into getting up, getting in the teacher's car, and being taken to the exam hall.

Many will have no intention of further involvement with the state education system, although come the autumn they will find themselves enrolled in some FE course through a variety of pressures. Most will have no ability or inten-tion to earn a living in any conventional way. At sixteen, they have become the young excluded. The process by which boys from unskilled working class back-grounds ensure social reproduction by rejecting educational success and electing for exploitative employment has been well described. Young people from the underclass go through a parallel process. There is no doubt that they have chosen their path. They have *chosen* exclusion.

The teachers who care

Do teachers collude in this process? From a sociological perspective, the answer must be, objectively, yes. Objectively, teachers are the agents through which the school performs its inevitable function of social reproduction and social selection in a stratified society. But, subjectively, oh how they struggle against it! This alienation from learning is the antithesis of everything they stand for, everything they themselves believe in so strongly. Even more, they would not be working in such schools without some social commitment, some desire to improve the lot of the deprived in our society. Otherwise, how could they stand it, day in, day out?

So, they struggle. In recent years, all kinds of methods have been used to rescue as many as possible. Frequently, the focus has been quite deliberately on those pupils in Years 10 and 11 who seem to be on the borderline between grades C and D at GCSE. These are the high achievers in the school, those who have most resisted the dominant practice of rejection, the silent minority who would prefer to pass some exams. This group is chosen not only because it is most likely to be productive, but because the 5 A-C grade measure is now of such public significance. Of course, adopting this approach sends a further message to the 90% of pupils not included. The existence of such a group in even the most difficult of our schools is another reminder that I do not intend to describe a social or cultural uniformity.

Such pupils are likely to benefit from a mentoring scheme. In essence, an adult who has the qualities and position to be a role model for the pupil visits the school on a regular basis to befriend, advise and counsel on an individual basis as the pupil struggles through the GCSE course. The mentor performs the role that would be performed by a parent in a middle class-family.

Alternatively or additionally, the pupil might benefit from an additional tutor on the staff. This would be an experienced teacher who would give extra sessions for guidance on aspects of study. Time management to allow suffi-cient study, organising work schedules, keeping work deadlines, helping to sort out problems with a particular subject or teacher, study skills, might be the kinds of issues dealt with in these sessions. The additional tutor will monitor the pupil's overall performance across the range of subjects, with the explicit aim of maximising the number of A-C grades. Obviously, organising and maintaining either an external mentoring or internal tutoring scheme is time-consuming. Even for this group, following up absence from sessions will occupy some time. It is generally considered, however, to be productive, assuming appropriate candidates are selected initially.

Many subject teachers will offer additional tuition in their subject, either explicitly or implicitly for the target group. This tends to be less successful, because attendance at such after-school sessions is sporadic, and it is difficult for the subject teacher to follow up absence. Nevertheless, a few individuals may benefit. Many teachers in all kinds of secondary schools give extra lessons as exams approach, but it does require extra commitment in the school for the underclass because of the exhaustion produced by the normal school day.

In short, these selected pupils will have as much positive attention as is possible within the constraints of the mayhem around them. All this effort, all these interventions, illustrate the point that even underclass schools are not social monoliths. Some of the pupils, perhaps a sizeable minority, are at least ambivalent about the idea of educational advance, qualifications, seeking to join the mainstream economy.

Such innovations also illustrate the considerable distance between reality and the pronouncements of government spokespersons. Teachers are fed up with hearing about 'big new ideas' which have been practised up and down the country for years. Breakfast clubs, homework clubs, revision centres, mentoring, and on and on: underclass schools have done them all. To see some of these highlighted as radical new thinking in Education Action Zones only increases the cynicism of those who believe that everything done by the government is mainly for media effect.

All this activity does make a difference. It makes a lot of difference to those individuals who achieve GCSE success and go on to other educational institutions where they are not so much of an oddity. It makes a difference to the school's GCSE statistics. But it should not be forgotten that this massive investment has been directed at a tiny minority of pupils. Perhaps it boosts the percentage gaining five A-C grades to 10%, or even 15%. In truth, the difference overall is marginal.

All of these efforts are directed outside the classroom, outside the normal lesson timetable. All of them are attempts to compensate for the fundamental absence of learning in the classroom. The lessons observed earlier provided little opportunity for learning except for the most independently minded pupils, and the teaching technique of the three Cs may seem unprofessional and uncommitted. Yet these same teachers routinely offer all kinds of support outside the lessons to any interested pupil. This is further evidence that the teaching style seen in the underclass school is forced on unwilling teachers by their pupils.

I have shown in this chapter that underclass secondary schools are a small but clearly identifiable group, with a great tendency to retain that status over many years. I have described how school life there is full of oppositional relationships, with resistance from pupils to all the normal routines which can be taken for granted in most schools in the country. I have shown how young members of the underclass elect for educational failure and exclusion, and how many teachers give unbounded commitment to winning back just a few of those who oppose or are suspicious.

It all reminds me, in a way, of those zealots who knock on suburban doors seeking to make religious conversions. No-one in such sects seems surprised at a low success rate, even though they must know of the huge gulf between their beliefs and the values and interests of those they seek. Neither do they seem downhearted by even the most brusque rejection. They just soldier on, content in saving even the ones and twos. Let us now see how the campaign looks to the soldiers in the education class war.

4

THE TEACHERS OF THE UNDERCLASS

A T THE START OF EVERY DAY, the teacher in the school for the under-class has one issue towering over every other aspect of the job. It is, which kids have I got today? Then, what mood will they be in? Will (there follows a list of the usual suspects) be totally uncontrollable? Those who do not believe that these are the big questions should look at the absence records of teachers in secondary schools. We may not approve, but we understand, why there is a correlation between the timing of sickness and the timetable for teaching the most difficult classes.

It's all relative, of course: the 'less difficult' classes would be beyond the pale thirty miles out of town. The problem is, this issue tends to be the great unmentioned cloud over the classroom. The fact is, the problem of class control is, well, not quite respectable within the education system. As I have implied, there are all kinds of reasons why all kinds of people want to keep quiet about it.

The taboo on disruption

It starts in teacher education and training. Until very recently, training in classroom management was an extremely marginal activity. Both in college and in supervision of teaching practice, the emphasis was overwhelmingly on the aims and content of the lesson. It was just not considered quite nice to focus on the fact that unless the class was orderly, little learning would take place regardless of the quality of the planned learning experience. It seems to have been assumed that the teacher tells pupils what to do, and they do it.

This is one origin of the idea that the way to create order is to provide a high quality lesson with pupils as active learners. Lucky students would receive from lecturers, or from colleagues on teaching practice, rather more practical help. Teaching is partly a craft, and there are techniques for well-disciplined classrooms, but the 'tips for teachers' side of training has always been left to chance.

I was one of the lucky ones. I could not count how many training courses I have attended since I became a teacher, but one, early in my career, was worth more than all the others put together. There, I learnt that there was lots of research on the best ways to develop class control. I learnt the importance of 'being on-task'. I learnt the need for consistent application of class rules. Most of all, I learnt the necessity of positive management, how to 'catch 'em being good', the appropriate ratio of praise to blame, the ostentatious celebration of success and the quiet review of failure. I learnt that the application of consistent schemes of reward, based on realistic targets and attractive rewards, could modify the behaviour of even the most disruptive pupil. The techniques I learnt then have stood me in good stead ever since.

Unfortunately, very few of my colleagues have ever had the same opportunity for this kind of professional development. Any teacher reading this will say that everyone knows these things. Unfortunately, knowing them in some general abstract way is not the same thing as understanding the precise practicalities of their application in the classroom. How many teachers routinely say, 'Some of you aren't paying attention', instead of saying, 'I see that nearly all of you are ready to start'? Most teachers have never been taught that the one is more productive than the other. Many of our elders and betters pretend that this is an unimportant issue, in comparison with other aspects of lesson delivery.

The second place where there is an absence of realism about class management is within the official discourse within many schools, even those where disorder is the order of the day. Informally, the problem is recognised. The staff room will be full of comments like '8MJ were absolutely dreadful today' — or words to that effect — or 'I feel that Karen Smith's inappropriate behaviour patterns are a major factor behind her lack of progress, as well as providing me with additional stress' — or words to *that* effect. However, these words are much more likely to be spoken by classroom teachers to their peers. It becomes more and more likely that care will be taken not to allow such sentiments to be overheard by management, since it might be taken as evidence of a lack of positive attitude, or a lack of competence.

Even in some schools for the underclass, there is a reluctance to accept that the behaviour of pupils in classes and the public places is a matter of policy, rather than a spin-off from improving the 'quality of teaching'. There is, of course, official discourse on the behaviour of individual pupils. As explained earlier, misbehaviour is always treated as an individual pathology, and staff will often work together on dealing with the individual. Only in extreme crisis will a whole class be treated as an object for co-operative analysis and action.

The official position seems to be that teachers are supposed to be skilled at managing classes. If they cannot cope, it is a reflection on their abilities, not the nature of the class, the lack of training, or the lack of an open debate on the general inability to cope.

The third place where there is a massive silence about pupil disorder and the near impossibility of controlling it in some places is the school's external relations. As I have continually stressed, a major motive for me in writing this book is to bring into the open that which is normally hidden, not only from government, but from parents, the community and the local authority. I have explained why this question has to be played down by schools in a competitive market. The truth about disorder is so much worse than these groups understand, but no school is in a position to be candid. This pressure only increases the reluctance to have a frank debate internally.

Doctor, doctor, the stress is killing me ...

So the tension, or fear, that dominates the teacher's psychology and physiology in the school for the underclass as the first bell approaches is for the most part a secret. Mixed in with this might well be an extreme tiredness, particularly towards the end of terms. Being in a room with a class of children is exhausting and stressful. Being there for five hours is extremely exhausting and stressful. Being there for five hours five days in a row is *killing*.

According to doctors and life insurance companies, teaching is now almost the most stressful occupation of all. Career teachers have a considerably reduced life expectancy, as compared with the general population, let alone as compared with the professional classes generally. No other task performed by teachers is nearly as exhausting and stressful as teaching a class.

Many teachers work not with classes, but with individuals or small groups. This has its own difficulties. Many teachers are promoted out of the classroom, to undertake administrative or managerial work. Modern headteachers rarely find the time to teach at all. To be honest, teachers often feel some resentment at all these colleagues, because whatever they are doing, and whatever the difficulties, they have it easier than those in classrooms.

There are various explanations for the promotion of teaching to the top of the occupational stress league, and no doubt a number of factors play their part. A large factor, however, is the problem of class control faced by most teachers. It is wearing to be ignored, disobeyed, or defied for twenty-five hours a week, particularly when the rules of engagement make turning the other cheek the mandatory response.

Unlike many jobs, teachers have no control over the timing of their performances. If they are having an off day, they cannot turn to other tasks, coming back to the difficult one when they feel better. They cannot take a day's leave if they feel like it. They cannot take a holiday when they feel run down. The end of long terms is characterised by problems caused by the exhaustion of the staff, and to a certain extent pupils too. At least a week is needed for recovery, and preparation time for the next term is also needed. This reality needs to be borne in mind when discussing the shape and size of the school year, and the apparently inordinate length of teachers' holidays.

So, the teaching day begins. In many schools in this country, each lesson is a battle. In the inner city, and the estates, only the extremely well organised and capable teachers will get a result, because resistance is substantial: and as I have shown, in the school for the underclass, only the superteacher will get a result, because the dominant attitude amongst the pupils is that the teachers are, indeed, the enemy.

In war, however, the troops are withdrawn between engagements for R&R. In school, there is no respite. As one lesson finishes, the next begins, with no more time than to put away one set of books and get out another. Unfinished business from one class must be put aside, the attention must be transferred without pause to the next class, and the concentration on hundreds more social interactions, many of them negative, must start again.

Breaks might be a time for relaxing with a coffee, but more likely a chance for a number of hurried arrangements with colleagues, looking at mail and memos received, and back to more of the same. What about the lunch hour? When I was young, in the lunch hour we expected to have something to eat, then chat in the staffroom. Conversation might range from immediate matters to more general discussion about education, football or fashion. Dreadful to recall, occasionally teachers actually left the site during the lunch hour!

Indeed, I always feel that some of my most effective teaching was during the period when the unions organised a work to rule and all the staff left the site every lunchtime. It is true I had the advantage of living opposite the school, but for that period I returned for the afternoon refreshed and ready to give of my best. In the same way, many older teachers will say they got some of their best results during the long-running dispute in the eighties, when we dropped other duties and concentrated only on teaching.

What do we find now? A visitor will find a staffroom almost empty during the lunch hour. Are they all at the pub? No, they are in their rooms and offices all over the building, beavering away, eating while they work, doing the paperwork they resent. What kind of preparation is this for the intense work of the afternoon? All too soon, the bell sounds again, and it's back to the fray.

The afternoon is a repeat of the morning. It must not be forgotten that for every moment of every lesson taught, the teacher needs total concentration, and indeed even then can never perceive everything going on. Apart from dozens of interactions simultaneously proceeding, a number of which the teacher will need to join, there is the need to monitor the time, to remember, and maybe revise, the lesson plan, to make difficult judgements on dealing with a rapid succession of, or simultaneously occurring, situations, all while keeping calm, refusing to react to provocation, and straining above all to retain an environment in which learning can take place.

The intensity of the effort is impossible to convey. At the same time, the teachers are continuing their own performances. Teachers are performers. They are slightly larger than life, because they have to hold an audience, as well as persuading it to become active. But teaching is not really like acting. Actors do not normally perform to an audience consisting largely of people who do not want to be an audience. They do not have to perform for five hours every day, and then rush into the foyer, conduct a survey of audience reaction, and spend hours evaluating the responses. Performing is emotionally draining, but performance is only part of the teacher's role in the classroom. In the afternoon, as in the morning, a lesson is followed by a lesson, and there is no break in the intensity.

In the underclass school, the non-contact period could be a life-saver, because it provides a small break. It is so precious to the exhausted performer. It is an opportunity to reduce the adrenaline levels, to follow up pupils and incidents, or perhaps to do some marking. Unfortunately, in many places, many of these periods for recovery are lost owing to the need to take the class of an absentee colleague.

Cover is a normal part of the working day in secondary schools, but is also normally resented. It is particularly demoralising in the school for the underclass. Cover is usually allocated at short notice, and disrupts teachers' work plans. With few exceptions, little teaching takes place in such lessons. The teacher may know neither the pupils, the subject, nor the syllabus, and can only introduce the work set in a mechanistic fashion. Cover is child-minding. When pressure is so great, it is very demoralising to have to alter plans to accommodate a task which is seen as valueless.

I know a large secondary school where there is virtually no cover by classroom teachers for their absent colleagues. Many years ago, the school trained its pupils that they should always have with them a book to read, or some other self-directed work, in case of the absence of an expected teacher. Any class in that condition is sent to the school hall. There, it is supervised by a rota of senior staff, including the headteacher, timetabled for that task. There is no pretence that the scheme of work is being followed, only for the returning teacher to find that the lesson must be repeated. The supervisor has to carry the authority to control what may become a large number of pupils, when many teachers are absent, but would expect to be able to continue with some administrative work while supervising. The school also continues to pay supply teachers to cover longer-term absence. The practice has had no noticeable negative effect on attainment; indeed, the school's results are improving faster than average.

The fact is, teachers are vaguely aware that their European colleagues, from countries whose attainments are frequently held up as targets for Britain, have no obligation to cover. British teachers resent it, and do not think it effective. There are many ways, some of them costing little as I have shown, in which it is possible to supervise children whose teacher is absent. This task should be taken from classroom teachers, particularly in underclass schools where the pressures of their other commitments are so immense.

Similar arguments attach to the requirement for British teachers, unlike their counterparts elsewhere, to supervise children outside the classroom. This might include periods at each end of the school day, during breaks, or when pupils are undertaking tests or exams. These duties take valuable time, increase the pressure on teachers, but make absolutely no contribution to pupil attainment. A very expensive resource is being misused for tasks which could be undertaken by other staff.

Performers do get booed off the stage on occasion. I do not know how they react, unless the stories of hitting the bottle are accurate. Teachers rarely retire to the staff room to get drunk in the middle of the school day. One of the five classes I observed ended with the teacher in tears. This is not rare. Even the strongest of us is close to tears after a lesson in which a substantial proportion of the class simply refused to attend to anything we said. Look closely in the underclass school, and you will see teachers shaking, struggling to speak coherently, almost dazed. There is no respite for them; shortly, they must go over the top again.

Many people who come to work in these schools simply walk out in the middle of their first day, or during their first week. Often, they have spoken to no-one; they simply go. None of the staff ask why. They know. Many more will last the term, or even a year, but then leave, for jobs which are not as damaging to their health.

Some, however, remain at the same school for many years. They work out their own strategies for coping with the pressures, they maintain their dedication to the communities they are serving, and they cope. Sad to say, many of these heroes go under eventually. In the end, the pressure tells, and they suffer varieties of breakdown. Of all the causes, the overwhelming one is the continual stress of confronting opposition in classrooms, five hours a day, five days a week.

... And the workload

One thing we can say about teaching in the school for the underclass is that the time does not drag. After rushing around without pause, suddenly it is the end of another exhausting day. Maybe there has been no incident, none of those confrontations which suck away irreplaceable chunks of emotional capital. Maybe it has just been an ordinary day of low-key contests of wills. Maybe there was even a high when one of the better classes was sufficiently controlled to get involved in a lesson, and discovered that the material so carefully prepared really was worth studying. But anyway, it's all over — for a few hours. The staff return to the staff room, and sag.

Except they cannot relax, because the working day is only half over for them. According to the research carried out periodically for the Pay Review Body, teachers work on average over fifty hours a week, less than half of which is spent actually teaching. What makes the hearts of teachers sink at 3.30 each day is the knowledge that they cannot do what they need to do, which is to have a sleep, but they have hours of work in front of them, some at school and some at home. Indeed, for many teachers, the remainder of their waking hours will be taken up by travel home, domestic responsibilities, and more work.

The pain is increased because the bulk of the work they are about to do is neither self-directed nor valued. To put it bluntly, although the situation varies from school to school, teachers may spend up to thirty hours each week on activities which are largely a waste of time. In many schools, it is this bitter fact which demoralises and exhausts as much as the stresses of the classroom. All this is felt by all teachers, but those who feel it most are those for whom the pupil contact hours are most demanding.

It is a strange and irrational phenomenon of the modern economy that there is a substantial proportion of adults who cannot find work, while at the same time those who are employed are required to work longer and longer hours. Officially, hours of work are reduced, but various forms of pressure produce unofficial overtime, unpaid of course. In Britain we work longer hours than anywhere else in Europe. Resistance to this pressure results in a dangerous accusation of lack of commitment to the organisation.

In professional and managerial jobs, working long hours is often some kind of status symbol, supposedly indicating that the employee is indispensable. Teachers who complain about their working hours are prone to being told to stop whinging, because longer hours are a fact of modern life, but I do not support the idea that because a plague has attacked many of the houses in my village, I should welcome its intrusion into mine. Whatever might be said about it in other occupations, working 51 hours a week (and rising) is bad for teachers and bad for their pupils. It leaves teachers too exhausted to be able to work at their best, and with too little time to pursue other lives outside the job that would make them more rounded people, and thus better teachers.

Some of the tasks are essential to the teaching process, particularly the preparation and follow-up to lessons. Their form varies according to the phase; in primaries, more emphasis is placed on displaying pupils' work, in secondaries, more on marking work done in exercise books. Both are very time-consuming. Proper marking and preparation might take 15 hours each week.

Unfortunately, teachers do not have 15 hours a week to spare. According to the Review Body, the average secondary teacher manages 8 hours of marking a week. I think a professional consensus would be that careful marking is an important contributor to pupil performance; even in the underclass school, many pupils peruse the marking, if only to contest the comment or the mark. This is one matter where all parties agree, but the evidence is that insufficient time is made available to teachers to do the job adequately.

The time needed for lesson preparation varies considerably according to two factors. The first is whether the aims and content of the lesson are new, or whether it has been taught many times previously. The second is the experience of the teacher. It is obvious that teachers starting on a career need to spend longer thinking through the aims, objectives, content, method and evaluation of a lesson. They will probably need to make detailed notes, which will be useful in future years, in the same way that was required during training. Experienced teachers, repeating a lesson taught often, might need only to spend a few minutes running through it in their minds, and checking the availability of resources.

Many teachers feel that the recent pressure to tighten up on the planning and preparation process has improved classroom practice, but in many primary schools, as well as secondary schools for the underclass when they have been placed in Special Measures by Ofsted, the process has become distorted.

Drowning in paper

In these schools, it is not the planning itself which is irksome, as much as the requirement for recording it. Teachers have to write out, in great detail, on standard forms, the aims of each lesson, the content, the materials and methods to be used, and an evaluation of the outcomes. The key to this immense waste of time is that the submission of all this paper is to management. For the first time, processes which had always been the property of the individual teacher, or of a team of teachers, have become the property of management.

Headteachers produce some weird and wonderful reasons why they need these hundreds of planning sheets. Many revolve round the 'supposing you dropped down dead tomorrow' scenario, suggesting that if teachers are absent, their replacement could use these planning sheets to ensure continuity. This ignores the virtually universal practice of teachers to set work in detail for any replacement teacher in the event of their absence.

The real reasons are much more simple and obvious. The headteachers can file the planning sheets. When the local or Ofsted inspectors call, the heads can hoist them out to prove that they are efficient managers and their staff are 'effective deliverers of the curriculum', as they say. The headteacher can also use them to monitor and discipline the staff, and in so doing create that ethos of monitoring and discipline which pervades the atmosphere of the failing school. It adds to the tendency toward management by bureaucracy, which is entirely inappropriate for school staff.

What managers really need to know is not how a lesson is planned, but how it works in practice, and what are the learning outcomes for the students. Pretending to monitor the latter through the former is a bureaucrat's cop-out. I have seen teachers whose plans were regarded as inadequate, but whose classroom performance was excellent. I have also seen teachers produce quite adequate plans even though their teaching in the classroom was disastrous. Planning, and its recording, ought to be for the benefit of the teachers who will be implementing the plans in the classroom. Teachers dare not say so, but the present requirements for evidence of planning amount to a denunciation of the staff, a denial of their professionalism and competence, and a degree of monitoring and control both unprecedented and unwarranted.

There are many other kinds of paperwork now demanded of teachers, and the load seems to be most onerous in the underclass school, particularly after it has failed its Ofsted inspection. Maintaining records on pupils is another task which is becoming an unreasonable extension of an otherwise necessary part of the job. Of course teachers need to know what their pupils have achieved, in order to plan further progress. Until fairly recently, however, teachers' markbooks were strictly their own, used in their own ways for their own purposes. To put it simply, teachers used their professional judgement about the most effective ways of recording the progress of their pupils.

In the course of a year, teachers build up huge banks of knowledge and understanding of the pupils in their care. Much of that bank is retained in their heads, because its only use is to guide their approach to the individuals and the class; no-one else has that responsibility, and no-one else needs that knowledge.

Now, however, we have the demand that everything is written down. Now, we have the whole school records policy. Now, teachers spend many hours writing down what they know about pupils and their attainments, in a standard format. The format might be produced by the local authority, or by the school (more reinventing the wheel).

In the case of pupils who are placed on the Special Educational Needs register under the SEN Code of Practice, the bureaucracy is particularly immense. Each pupil must have an Individual Education Plan, and the teachers must record every breath and movement towards meeting the targets within it. In the underclass school, the overwhelming majority of pupils would meet the criteria for entry on the register, but that is impracticable. Usually, the SEN Co-ordinator selects about that half of the pupils who are most in need.

IEP records are used within the statutory process of review laid down by the Code of Practice, but what happens to most pupil records? They are filed. The theory is that the record can be transferred to a pupil's new teacher, in other classes, or in a new school. The reality is that the record is filed. Teachers who want to know more about a pupil who is new to them will do the obvious thing and ask their colleagues. A three-minute conversation will reveal far more than a ten-minute search in the filing cabinet followed by a perusal of some standardised information.

A particularly obvious example of this phenomenon is the transfer of records from primary to secondary schools. The secondary teacher with pastoral responsibility will go to those files when a pupil becomes troublesome, and it is helpful to know the 'previous'. Any other secondary teacher will look up those records only very rarely.

Those pundits who will denote me a dinosaur will claim that improving the quality of the records we keep on our pupils is an important contribution to improving their performance. My answer is that any gain is completely disproportionate to the work involved, and that the very great majority of words written by tired underclass teachers during their evenings are never read by anyone.

The question is, who needs to know, and what? We now have, at four stages in compulsory education, nationally set assessments which produce standard information on individual attainment in a range of subjects. Since one of the purposes of the education system is to produce a differentially qualified cohort of young people, sorted for entry to the workforce, standard qualifications are essential.

The issue is one of balance, of utility. We have been told a thousand times that weighing the pig produces no extra pork, and educationists from abroad are perplexed at the assessment overkill within the English system. However, nobody pretends that these national assessments are primarily for educational purposes. They are not intended as diagnostic tools to inform the further development of the child, but as indicators for the education market established by the 1988 Act. The justification is that parents need to know, not so much about the progress of their own child, but the market situation of schools.

What parents want to know probably varies a great deal, according to their class and other factors. In the underclass school, all kinds of work will be done to gain the interest, and perhaps the commitment, of antagonistic and suspicious parents. Even here a minority of parents retain hope for their offspring. They generally want to know how their child is progressing in comparison with the class, but do not want to know a mass of detail. Their teachers are forced to provide them, however, with hundreds of words explaining just what topics have been covered in each subject, what skills and concepts have been learnt. Walk the streets around the underclass school after these reports to parents have been given to pupils to take home. The gutters are littered with them.

Despite that, teachers will feel obliged to hold yet more meetings, this time to explain to parents what the forthcoming Key Stage tests mean, and how to interpret the results. What the parents really want to know is whether their child seems happy and is well-behaved.

I have a confession here. In the old days, when records for parents consisted of an annual report with a small piece of paper for each subject, I used to enjoy report-writing. Now I know this makes me seem an oddity to my colleagues, but for me it was a challenge to find a few words which summarised each pupil's character, behaviour, and work in my lessons. It was, in fact, an intellectual game. The one thing of which I was always aware as I spent many happy hours on this game was that it was strictly for my own benefit. Perhaps, just perhaps, one of my colleagues who would collate and check the reports would read the report and, I hoped, would chuckle or nod. Some of the older and more committed pupils would want my judgement. A few of the parents would read it and, having read it, would move on. I enjoyed it while knowing it had absolutely no value at all in terms of the learning process.

What were far more valuable were the pupil reports on me, because I would distribute report blanks and ask the class to assess my performance over the year — strictly between them and me, of course. Now that was a useful exercise in appraisal. I wouldn't do it now, of course; one of the reports might fall into the wrong hands and be used against me.

Whether it is records designed for use by teachers, or records for parents or others, there is now in our schools a complete lack of balance about the value of the work in comparison with the time spent. I conclude that the reason for this development is the same as for the requirement for records of planning. It is an instrument of surveillance and control. The paper has to be there. If anyone, an inspector say, asks the headteacher, the reply is, 'Here are our pupil records, this is our policy, we are efficient and effective.'

The existence of all these records is of little relevance to school effectiveness, and is evidence of inefficiency, at least in the prioritisation of teacher time, but the inspector is happy. The headteacher is happy. If the paper from a particular teacher is not there, the headteacher is unhappy. The headteacher has another stick, another note in the teacher's file, another brick in the wall of management by harassment. It all goes to make life in the underclass school that bit more unbearable.

Meetings and management

The other form of useless work is the meetings. Meetings are endemic in our schools, but tend to be even more numerous in the underclass school, where they add yet more pressure at the end of the school day.

There might be meetings of the whole staff, departments, pastoral teams, so-called senior management teams, middle management teams, working parties, and a whole range of one-off meetings for various purposes. Naturally, those who call the meetings profess them to be important. Many of them are in fact quite unnecessary.

They are used to circulate routine information, which could be achieved more efficiently by means of a written notice. They are used to create the impression of consultation on decisions which have been taken by management. They are used to develop policy by committee, which could be drafted more efficiently by an individual.

Most headteachers feel they need to play safe by having available for Ofsted inspectors carefully worked and reworked statements of policy on every conceivable aspect of school life. Never mind that inspectors are far more interested in practice than policy, the keen headteacher delivers boxes of paperwork to the team. The team, up against severe time constraints as a result of the bidding regime, will never read the papers.

The question is, who did the working and the re-working of these policy statements? Well, any head knows that the staff need to feel they have 'ownership' of the policies, and ownership can only be engendered by studying and revising drafts in groups for hour after hour. The only question not asked in the meeting is, 'Is this a waste of time, or will it benefit my teaching and my pupils' learning?' That question is reserved for the moaning session suffered by the teachers' households when they finally get home. The answers tend to be yes, and no, in that order.

Some schools only hold staff meetings when necessary. Almost all schools hold some staff meetings which are useful. Unfortunately for the workloads of teachers, however, most schools hold a lot of staff meetings which are of no benefit, or whose benefits could be achieved more efficiently by other means.

In far too many schools, headteachers call meetings without asking themselves whether they are the best use of that most scarce resource, teacher time. Indeed, the open-ended teacher's contract discourages headteachers from ever considering that teacher time is a scarce resource at all. It is easy to imagine the effect on morale when teachers haul themselves in numb exhaustion from their rooms at the end of the day to a staff meeting, only to sit there fuming at its uselessness and remembering all the tasks remaining to be done before the day is out.

People who have worked elsewhere before becoming teachers are more able than most to evaluate the way schools manage their staffs. In my experience, they always deplore the flabbiness. Calling meetings is one result of two fatal weaknesses in most of our schools, whether or not they serve the underclass.

The first is a failure of the delegation of authority. Rarely are tasks and duties allocated to individuals accompanied by the authority to complete them. Staff are expected to consult up and down the artificial hierarchy now created in even the smallest school. How do we consult? Why, we hold a meeting, of course — if not two or three.

There is no doubt that teachers are their own worst enemies in this respect. Most of us want to do things just exactly the way we think. We spend hours preparing our own teaching materials because those available are not exactly what we want. We want every school document just the way we want it. So we simply cannot let a colleague with responsibility get on with the job. Most school managements are part of this culture, and cannot give staff the autonomy to do their jobs.

The second weakness is indecision. When faced with the need to make a decision, many headteachers call a meeting to discuss it. I believe that in other cases the real purpose of the meeting is to give added legitimacy to a decision already made. In some schools, there is a feeling that management ought to be by 'democracy', by acting on the majority view of the staff on every issue.

I received a valuable lesson in this, very early in my career. The head had told a packed staff meeting his attitude to a particular matter, and made to leave. With the arrogance of youth, I challenged him to take a vote. For a moment he looked at me with a mixture of annoyance and pity that I understood so little. 'I have to tell you, Mr. Johnson,' he said, 'that if 116 members of staff were to vote one way, and I voted the other, then I would have won the vote by a small majority.' Then he left the room.

A school would need few staff meetings if responsibilities, and the authority to make decisions within that area of responsibility, were shared. In the present hierarchical structure, however, few headteachers do delegate in this way. Instead, they call meetings.

Who's heaping it on?

Following pressure from the unions, the government has issued a circular advising schools to cut down on unnecessary paperwork and meetings. At the same time, other branches of the same government continue to bombard schools with new requirements for paperwork and meetings. While the arguments continue around Whitehall, in the overwhelmed schools for the underclass, teachers misuse hours of their time every week on these fruitless tasks which only exhaust them more, and which offer nothing to the pupils who need so much. How does this come to be? Who is forcing this load on them?

The orders are given directly by the headteachers. One of the many damaging effects of the Education Reform Act, with its highly centralised and prescriptive national curriculum linked with its highly decentralised local management of schools, is the subversion and transformation of the role of headteacher.

First, they are now given, in effect, the statutory duty to comply with a curriculum over which they have absolutely no control, and which is criticised by them as much as in other educational circles.

Second, although the Ofsted regime is detested by all, it is headteachers who know that they are number one in the firing line after an adverse inspection report, and the resultant fear informs everything they do.

Third, they are now required to think of their schools as small businesses, without having any significant opportunity to influence significantly their income or expenditure without gross distortion of their aims, and in an environment of resource reduction.

Fourth, they are constantly exhorted to consider themselves 'managers', and are required to take on a whole series of financial, personnel, site management and other roles, entirely without any training, and virtually without support.

Local management has given most headteachers power over their staff without any effective checks or balances. Few governing bodies can develop an appropriate relationship with their heads, whom they oversee in an independent but supportive style without excessive interference in everyday management. No wonder that heads feel they need to work sixty hours a week and more; no wonder it becomes more and more difficult to recruit heads for underclass schools, even with ever inflating salary offers; no wonder that many of those who do come forward these days are psychologically inclined towards all the worst excesses of an outdated 'carrot and stick without the carrot' approach to management.

So headteachers are under external pressures as never before. The large majority, understandably, cope by transmitting and amplifying the pressures to the staff as a whole. This is the direct source of the really useless work that teachers are now required to do. Most teachers, however, recognise that the head is only passing on pressures from outside. They blame Ofsted, above all, for originating the pressure. In Chapter 5, I describe just how the famed brown envelope announcing a forthcoming Ofsted inspection creates a full-scale alert — except in schools where 'far-sighted' heads realise well in advance that the threat of an eventual inspection can be used to justify all sorts of extra work. Notwithstanding the massive books of guidance about Ofsted inspections, there is widespread insecurity about what the inspectors will be seeking. This is not helped, of course, by the very wide variations in practice and standards of judgement between inspection teams.

A mythology arose, early in the first cycle of inspections, that the inspectors required every aspect of school life to be recorded on paper. Untold boxes of paperwork were delivered to the inspectors, even though the severe time constraints prevented them from ever being read. Ofsted, however, for a long time did nothing to deny the myth. Her Majesty's Chief Inspector of Schools has created a climate of intimidation by his public pronouncements, and of course the inspection is the mechanism of enforcement. An interesting question for students of government is the degree to which Ofsted should be seen as an autonomous body, and conversely the degree to which it is more accurately seen as the agent of government. There is a spread of opinion about this amongst teachers, but for the majority Ofsted is the demon, and the DfEE gets off lightly.

I do not see things that way. Government established Ofsted, it appoints its leader; government could reform or abolish Ofsted. It suits government that Ofsted has the appearance of autonomy, and by appointing the 'right' HMCI whose agenda is largely that of the government, it can permit apparent autonomy. I think teachers should see Ofsted for what it is, a mechanism for implementing the government's education policies, and should redirect their anger.

Teachers are a very large and economically significant sector amongst public servants. In recent times, governments have shown a particular interest in both pay and work output for teachers, with imposed national terms and conditions. The government is entitled to intervene to improve educational standards, and will inevitably attempt to require ever more work from us. Teachers need to see government as the originator of their work-load problems, and resistance to government as the only way to reduce them.

Demoralised and exhausted

The government now realises that its educational aims will be obstructed if teacher morale continues to be low. It is far from clear that the government understands why morale is low, particularly in the inner city. Hence this book.

There are a number of inter-related causes of demoralisation, often rehearsed in the education press. The constant public criticism must not be under-rated as one. In September 1997, the Prime Minister was the first holder of that office to address the TUC for nineteen years. Speaking to representa-tives of nearly 7 million employees, his theme was the need for unions to modernise. Yet even in such a place, at such a time, with such a theme, he mentioned just one occupational group — teachers. His only comment was a demand for action against incompetents.

What kind of balance is this? It seems like monomania. It sounds like cheap short-term populism. It is damaging to the education system, because of the demoralisation it produces. It is evidence that the government is running education as a vote-catching enterprise, with decisions based on short-term political advantage rather than the needs of the service. The perception of this is another demoralising factor for teachers.

The growth in job insecurity is another. This is produced by two different trends. The first is the tendency to employ teachers on temporary contracts, or to use agency staff, particularly in the London area. The second is the growth in redundancy, which is the direct result of the introduction of local management. The figures for compulsory redundancy underestimate the salience of the issue, because the large majority of schools which announce the need for staffing reductions achieve them by more or less voluntary means, but the fear of redundancy has now entered the collective conscious-ness of teachers.

Many other factors produce demoralisation. However, I believe that the most important is the one I have been describing in this chapter. Whatever anyone may say to justify the present arrangements, teachers are fed up with the amount of work they are expected to do, the constant additions, the lack of facilities they have to do it, and what they see as the pointlessness of much of it. They are fed up with the degree to which they are monitored, checked and inspected in ways that demean them as professionals and are quite out of balance with the proper need for their work to be accountable. In the underclass school, above all, they are also fed up and worn out by the stress of coping with difficult children.

There is no doubt that teachers in very large numbers suffer what can only be described as burn-out. I believe that human beings are born with a finite amount of what I call emotional capital, the resources to cope with difficult situations. Some have more than others, of course, and a person specification for teaching includes a large stock of emotional capital. In the school for the underclass, the pressures I have described, and in particular the daily confrontation with aggressive recalcitrance, use huge reserves of emotional capital. Of those who stay, most suffer sooner or later. These days, I meet far too many teachers of the underclass who have been made ill by the job, who have worked themselves into the ground on behalf of the nation's most deprived young people.

It is not appropriate to explain these breakdowns in terms of individual pathologies. The frequency is simply too great, and too unpredictable. Some of the underclass teachers who collapse are the strongest, the most dynamic, the most charismatic; they just run out of emotional capital.

This phenomenon raises the question of whether teaching in the underclass school is mission impossible. The government must ask itself whether this kind of school, in its present form, is an intrinsically failing institution, where survival is beyond the powers of ordinary mortals. At the same time, it must understand that simple closure is not the answer, because the status will be transferred with the pupils to another school.

Recruitment: the revolving door

In total, the staffing situation in the underclass school is one of permanent crisis. There will be a core of teachers who have been there for a number of years, including some senior staff who have lasted more than a decade. Without this core, the school would collapse completely. Yet, from time to time, it is depleted by breakdown, or by escape before too late.

Then there is a group of teachers, mostly young, many perhaps in their first posts, who have come through the initial period of shock, and are sticking it out for a while. A few will last long enough to join the essential core group, but most will do their five years and move on. This group has energy but little experience, but reminds me of the First World War trenches full of battle hardened old men of nineteen. There is also the large group of those who decide very soon after arrival that the school is not for them, and leave within days, or perhaps within the year.

Those who arrive as Newly Qualified Teachers (NQTs) are trying to learn their trade in the most impossible conditions. They may be employed because they are cheaper than older staff, or because they are the only applicants for vacancies, but it is in no-one's interests to have such a group thrown in to such a school. The government's proposal to ban failing schools from taking on NQTs is good in itself, but it will further increase the difficulties of finding staff.

Perhaps the largest single group of posts, however, is those which are vacant. Vacancies arise in underclass schools with great frequency, many at short notice. Vacancies may last many months, because it is difficult to find teachers who are prepared to work there. Advertisements attract a few enquiries; perhaps someone will be persuaded to come to an interview, but repeatedly, particularly in the shortage subjects, no-one can be persuaded to start. Or someone starts, and stops very soon. Is it surprising that the same phenomenon is now affecting the headship of these schools? Ever larger salaries are offered, but no candidates come forward. The school for the underclass, increasingly, is characterised by the lack of a headteacher and a large proportion of the staffing complement.

In addition to the vacant posts, a large proportion of the staff will be absent. Some will be on long-term sick leave with stress-related conditions such as depression, and will never return. Staff in the underclass school also have higher than average rates of short-term sickness. The particular exhaustion produced by the job makes them more susceptible to illness, and when they wake up feeling under the weather they are more likely than other teachers to be deterred from going in by the prospect of their day ahead. Some will be absent from class because of other duties: attending a case conference, perhaps, or some other meeting arranged externally.

In the underclass school, the vacant posts and absent staff will comprise at least a quarter of the staffing complement. In other words, every day a quarter of the timetables need to be covered.

The gaps are filled by supply staff. By definition, these are teachers who prefer to work on a casual basis, so that pupils are confronted with a constantly changing figure in front of them. Continuity is essential for progression in any classroom, but for underclass children stability is absolutely vital. They will not respond in any way to teachers they do not know, and up to a half of the teachers they face will be new or transient or both.

With luck, the school can find a supply teacher who will fill the vacancy on a regular basis until a permanent appointment is made, but often a string of different people will come and go. In London, many of these are visitors from abroad on working holidays. One of the classes I describe in Chapter 7 had experienced twelve different teachers in the subject in the two years before I took them over, and that is by no means unusual.

Every day, every class will be taught once or twice by someone who does not know them, the school, or the systems. This is the most destabilising factor of all. Any professional will testify that knowing the pupils is essential. For one thing, unless you can call pupils by name, it is very difficult to gain their attention. 'You, stop talking' does not work: 'Darren, stop talking' just might.

It is generally accepted that high staff turnover rates in any organisation signal some problems within it. It is true that the highest turnover occurs in those underclass schools not blessed with superheads, but with ordinary head-teachers whose skills are insufficient for the mission impossible. Yet annual turnover of between a quarter and a third is typical of even the well-led school for the underclass. This alone would make effective education virtually impossible.

The crisis in teacher recruitment and retention is a national issue. I have argued in this chapter that the problems of classroom management, of work-load, of related stress, make recruitment and retention problematic in the school for the underclass irrespective of solutions which might be found for schools in general. No matter what incentives might be invented to attract staff to these schools, the job itself cannot be sustained by the large majority of those who try.

There are two possible reactions to this. The one I support is to conclude that the schools themselves must be reformed radically. The other, currently the policy, is to punish the schools for failing, to berate the teachers for incompetence, and to mount ever increasing pressure for improvements. This immensely damaging and ultimately futile response is operated by the Ofsted regime, which I examine next.

5

THE BIG 'O'

S CHOOLS WHICH CATER LARGELY FOR THE UNDERCLASS are qualitatively different from the vast majority. Yet the realities of life in such schools do not seem to be recognised by the current national inspection apparatus. Let us examine in more detail the Ofsted system, asking why it is ineffective in carrying out the task set for it by government, and in particular why it fails to provide any solutions for underclass schools.

It is not accidental that teachers call Ofsted 'the big O'. It has the same aura as does 'the big C' amongst consumers of medical services. It is feared and dreaded. If you have it, the outcome is perceived as almost inevitable, though there may be a long and very painful struggle first. Ofsted is regarded by all teachers in every school as a steamroller which is impossible to resist, even though it is immensely damaging to both teachers and the school.

It is possible to find a few headteachers who make public statements praising the utility of the inspection, but such statements are widely derided. The reality may not quite fit the anticipation. Recovery from some cancers is now commonplace. Not all schools find the inspection intolerable. So are teachers hysterical about Ofsted? Shouldn't they be like other professionals, and accept that it is proper for their performance to be assessed? Isn't Ofsted a vital tool for opening schools to public scrutiny, and thereby applying proper pressure on them to ratchet up their achievement? This chapter attempts to answer those questions from the perspective of a teacher.

The Ofsted inspection is a completely new phenomenon. Its first cycle finished in the summer of 1997. The independent review of its work showed... well, it showed nothing, because there has been no such investigation of whether this novelty is effective, in terms of the aims set for it by government. Given that Ofsted costs over £150 million a year, it is somewhat surprising that its claims for itself have not been scrutinised. Naturally, that did not prevent the new government from making unsubstantiated assertions, claiming that Ofsted was an essential part of schools' improvement process, and had improved performance by clearly identifying strengths and weaknesses. It also laid great stress on the 'vast databank of information'.

Ofsted's purpose

First of all, we need some clear thinking about the purposes of inspection in schools. One is to build and renew a national picture of what schools are doing, presumably in order to guide policy. As stated, the government sees that as a primary function of Ofsted. However, the method used is the general census: every school in the country is observed, in an intensive way, for as many characteristics as possible, and the observations are presented in the form of statistics. At any one time, the oldest elements of this database will be six years old, given the new six-year cycle of inspection.

I am inclined to believe that if researchers were given the brief, they would come up with a very different model of investigation. It would be far more cost-effective, and just as accurate, to work by sampling. Given a population of 25,000 schools, a stratified sample of 1200 schools should be sufficient. No doubt, some of the inspections would need to be general ones of the whole institution. However, using a sampling technique, it would be possible to focus on a particular aspect of school organisation, pedagogy, or whatever, and obtain reliable data on that topic reasonably quickly. For this purpose, then, perhaps the Ofsted model is lumbering and inefficient.

A second purpose, different from the first but often conflated, might be to discover the characteristics of individual schools. What for? Who needs this information? The answers are by no means clear. Leaving aside, for a moment, the tiny proportion of schools which are judged failing, since central government does not intervene at the level of the individual school, it does not need that degree of detailed information. This suggests a local use, either for the school, its parents, or the local authority.

On the one hand, we have the notion that parents ought to be told about local schools, partly in order to assist their choice of school. There are a number of problems with the idea that Ofsted reports are an essential component of that process.

First of all, under the highly prescriptive regulations now governing this kind of thing, schools are already under an obligation to publish all kinds of information. Parents have access to Key Stage results, public exam results, attendance figures, school policies on this, that, and the other, the governors' annual report. This is quite apart, of course, from detailed reports on the progress of their own children. Prospective parents have a prospectus. Parents in cities, who have a real choice of a number of schools, could be smothered in paper before they ever reached the Ofsted reports.

And when they did? The current official language of Ofsted is gobblede-gook. There is no possibility at all that any report so far written could provide any intelligible information to any but a tiny minority of parents. I have already pointed out that parental images of schools are created by a complex series of events, in which local gossip and observation play a significant part. Even exam results, are of minor significance. There is no evidence that Ofsted reports are themselves of any use — although, in some cases, an Ofsted label does matter.

On the other hand, inspection information might be of use to the local education authority. The government has made clear that the LEA will continue to have the function of monitoring the performance of its schools. A simple person might ask here, Why should we need a national inspection system when it has to be duplicated at local level? The question might become more urgent when we realise that Ofsted does not communicate in any way with LEAs about their schools.

A possible answer is that Ofsted inspectors are the most experienced, authoritative and respected body of professionals, who can exercise a validating function on local inspection. Unfortunately, this picture of Ofsted inspectors is far from the truth. As we shall see later, local inspectors and Ofsted inspectors are the same people in different hats. The Ofsted army is so large that all hands are needed for the pumps. It is little wonder that Ofsted has substantial problems of quality control amongst its inspectors. It simply cannot be said that the judgements of an Ofsted team are more authoritative than those of the local authority. Since it is difficult to see how a local authority can perform its statutory functions without a local inspection team, we must conclude that Ofsted is indeed an expensive duplication, in terms of its second possible purpose.

Oh, yes, there is one other possible purpose of school inspection: to provide specific help to schools to improve their performance. I wonder whether the reader shares my incomprehension that the one thing Ofsted inspections specifically will *not* do is to provide *any advice whatsoever* to the inspected school on how to improve.

What do they provide? The inspectors come, they see, they judge, they report: x% of teaching satisfactory, y% of learning satisfactory, this sound, that weak. They write a list of key points for action. They go away. The end. There is some discussion in the profession about the value of Ofsted reports. Some senior staff say they do provide insights which are new, and therefore help them plan. The vast majority of heads and other teachers, however, claim that the report tells them nothing they did not know already. And in some cases the inspectors get things completely wrong, either in fact or in judgement.

Whatever the quality of the report, the school is supposed to respond. The governors must prepare an action plan on the basis of the inspection's points for action, and the staff must then implement the action plan. There is no further guidance for the school on how to do any of that. Research indicates that schools are likely to implement only elements of the action plan which are simple, or which coincide with their own previous priorities.

It is important to note that there is absolutely no external monitoring of this phase of the process, unless by the local authority. In the experience of teachers, except in failing schools, when Ofsted has gone everybody heaves a sigh of relief and gets back to normal. Teachers' practice has not been affected because the inspectors do not tell them what elements of their work are good, what are poor, or advise them on ways to change their individual practice.

This is, in fact, the key complaint of teachers about Ofsted. All that expense, all that bureaucracy, all those hundreds of hours of work preparing for the inspection, all that stress — and for what? At the end of it, I have been told nothing about my work; I have had virtually no opportunity to discuss it; I have received no training of any kind; I have been given no opportunity to learn how to work more effectively. I am just where I started, except for the contribution to grey hair and burn-out.

Since September 1997, the regulations have required oral feedback, and it does happen sometimes. Usually, however, the inspector is going through some minimal motions — 'Your work is generally satisfactory' — and sometimes does not even manage that.

Why is a useful evaluation so seldom offered? The answer, in a word, is cash. Contracts to inspect schools are awarded, school by school, by tender. Her Majesty's government's Chief Inspector is proud that he is saving the country money by forcing down the price of an inspection, allegedly from about £20,000 to £17,000 on average for a secondary school. This is also forcing Ofsted teams to cut corners. The truth is that, in the current system, inspectors just do not have the time to observe teachers for a sufficient length of time, and certainly do not have the time to spend talking about what they have seen. They have time only to note their observations before moving on to the next class.

I insist: as a generalisation, teachers are not conservative. More or less willingly, they comply with demands from others to work in new ways. As fad follows fad, they go along with new teaching methods, new class organisation, new resources. The old hands just smile to themselves when the next innovation takes them forward to the orthodoxy of thirty years before, and get on with it.

What angers them about the current situation is that, for the first time, they are being told they must raise the attainment levels of their pupils without being told how they can do that. It's as if the British sporting public was saying to Tim Henman, 'Being in the top 20 isn't good enough. We want you ranked higher. By the way, we're not going to allow you any coaches or trainers, you've just got to work out for yourself how to get there. And you certainly haven't got the time to watch other top players for tips. Stop whinging and just get on with it. Oh, and sorry your practice court is cracked and worn, but we can't afford to do anything about it.'

I am forced to conclude that the present regime is an ineffective tool for any of the educational purposes it might serve. There is only one other explanation for Ofsted: that its purpose is almost entirely political.

Ofsted was set up as part of a government campaign against the so-called educational establishment, embodied in what was wittily called at the time the Great Reform Act of 1988. It provided, for the first time, a national system of inspection. The government could claim that it was showing determination to crack down on incompetent teachers and failing schools.

Ever since, Ofsted has been wheeled out whenever it has been politically expedient to appear decisive. Another set of unfavourable international comparisons? Ofsted to the rescue! — of the government, of course. A row over disruptive pupils? Ofsted will sort it out — the government spin, that is. Time for an attack on local government? Ofsted can target a few authorities.

Her Majesty's Inspectorate, which preceded Ofsted, had an impeccable record of independent judgement and action. It was independent of local authorities, teacher interests, and, particularly, the government of the day. Its judgements were respected all the more. The 'HMI' was incorporated, largely unhappily, into the Ofsted structure, and retains a distinctive role. In particular, it has significant responsibilities in failing schools. A team of HMI must visit such schools, firstly to confirm or otherwise the findings of the inspection team, secondly to monitor the recovery, and thirdly to carry out re-inspections at intervals until the school is judged to require special measures no longer. There is not the slightest pretence that Ofsted is independent of government, and its judgements are respected all the less.

The ideological work of Her Majesty's Chief Inspector, who should be retitled Her Majesty's Government's Chief Inspector, is only possible because he can claim the authority of thousands of school inspection reports as a database. The database is a fraud of gigantic proportions, but with the benefit of the Big Assertion, he can produce the statistic to suit any occasion.

There is another possible political use of Ofsted. Perhaps this seems far-fetched, but when I see the effects of the system on teachers, it looks suspiciously like an instrument of terror. Some of my colleagues see it as a reprisal for events in the eighties. The miners took on the Thatcher state; they and their industry were obliterated in revenge. The teachers took on the

Thatcher state; we came away with some losses, but intact. We even had the nerve to come back for another bite in the nineties, and managed to overturn some aspects of the national curriculum.

Ofsted certainly feels like a terror weapon. What other explanation could there be for the extraordinary length of notice given to schools about an inspection? I believe that inspectors should give the same notice as is polite for any other visitors to the school, say one or two weeks, rather than two years, or the current two terms. At a stroke, this would remove the Ofsted preparation stone from teachers' necks.

Another feature of Ofsted is its insulation from the rule of law. For example, it has a procedure for inserting schools into the inspection cycle. But when it suits, it ignores its own procedures by inspecting at short notice, or even without notice.

The following story may not be common, but it happened. An inspector turned up at a school one day and asked to look round. The headteacher was surprised, but said nothing; you don't say no to the men from Ofsted. Then he said he'd be back tomorrow with a colleague. On the third day, he came with another colleague. At the end of that day, he saw the headteacher and said words to the effect that their visit had been a formal Ofsted inspection. And an inspection it was. This behaviour was in absolute disregard of its own normal procedures. It was also quite obviously politically motivated, because the school had become notorious shortly before, with highly publicised industrial action by the teachers.

This example also illustrates another way in which Ofsted is above the law. It is almost impossible to challenge its behaviour, judgements or findings. According to its procedures, a headteacher is allowed an opportunity to correct any errors of fact before a report is completed. Sometimes errors are corrected, sometimes they are not. There was no mechanism for appeal against any decision or judgement, and Ofsted traditionally refuses to discuss such matters.

A simple example within my own experience: a primary school suffered a visit from an inspector at short notice, and a subsequent adverse report, almost a year after a very satisfactory report of a full inspection, and with no intervening change of circumstances. Why? The relevant Ofsted official refused to discuss with anyone why this had happened, let alone why the judgement should have altered.

Some time ago, one particular inspector became so notorious for incompetence and unprofessional conduct that the complaints reached the attention of the national press. Ofsted refused to discuss the complaints, or to reveal what, if any, action it had taken. Ofsted refuses to explain its interventions in schools which are outside the routine of inspection. Ofsted is, in fact, a law to itself.

The effects of this are twofold. Firstly, the reliability of its inspection evidence is diminished, because errors of observation may not be corrected. Secondly, the reign of terror is intensified by the knowledge that the O-men might appear at any time, might ransack your room, might write anything, without any restraint or redress. Ofsted often appears capricious, always seems unaccountable, and never seems impartial. That is why the nation's teachers are terrorised.

The government has now appointed an Independent Complaints Adjudicator. It is too early to know whether, in time, this will increase confidence that Inspectors are accountable. There has been no such confidence in the past.

How Ofsted preparation can damage the school

A little publicised feature of the current system, but well-known within the profession, is the disruption it causes to children's education. How can this be? Schools' understandings of how to prepare for an inspection have developed as the cycle has progressed, and the focus has changed from the construction of school policies to paperwork recording classroom activity.

Nevertheless, the school makes ever-increasing demands for extra administrative work in the months before the inspection. All the teachers are required to produce countless trees of information. New policies will be proposed, debated, redrafted and introduced on a range of teacher activity. Termly plans, weekly plans, daily plans, requiring minute detail of the planning and outcome of each and every lesson taught; assessment and marking policies, requiring the attainments of every pupil to be recorded in every detail and uniformly; in primary schools there will be a display policy, which determines when, how often and what materials are put up on the walls of each classroom and corridor, and may well resolve the vexed issue of double or triple mounting. (For those unaware of this technical argument, it is the question of the appropriate number of layers of backing paper needed to produce an attractive presentation of a piece of display material. Using the wrong number could be a disciplinary matter.)

As the forests are felled, the workload increases. How do the pupils suffer? It is commonplace, perhaps almost universal, that in the approach to an Ofsted teachers cancel the extra-curricular activities they normally offer. Whether it be sport, the arts, or other cultural activities; whether it be a long-standing organised club, or an informal gathering of like minds; the message goes out, sorry kids, no club this term, too busy.

A typical and telling example was provided for me by a highly experienced and professional colleague, not one easily panicked by authority, working with a headteacher who is also skilled, balanced, and not panicked by such as Ofsted. Not a P.E. teacher, this man had run an after-school basketball club for 26 years without a break. Had he taken part in the prolonged industrial action of the eighties? Yes, with enthusiasm. But he always found a way of keeping his club going (another myth bites the dust). Had he nothing else to do? He has an exceptionally time-consuming senior post within the school, and plenty of outside interests. Still, every week, for 26 years, he offered something extra to his pupils, until this magnificent record of service to young people was ended the term before his school's Ofsted. The paperwork just became too much.

Pupils also suffer in the classroom. The preparation and delivery of lessons during the run-up to Ofsted suffers because of the concentration on the other paperwork. In the last few weeks, in particular, 'keep 'em quiet' work may be set. In many primary schools, two or three weeks before O-day the headteacher will ask for copies of the plans for every lesson to be taught during the inspection week, and these will be reviewed and revised, materials meticulously planned. Many normal activities will be suspended for that week because they will not provide 'good experiences' for the O-men.

Does it sound like the build-up to Opening Night of some major production? That is certainly what it feels like. Normal service is suspended for months beforehand, and is not resumed until some time afterwards. Teachers would not accept this situation, which is so stressful for them and disruptive for their pupils, if they were not terrorised into compliance.

Many, many teachers and schools find their inspections to be ordinary experiences. All workers will feel some tension when their work is being judged, but apart from that, the week itself is not unpleasant, particularly when compared with the months leading up to it. Many schools are never the victim of sudden intervention. Yet even in such lucky places, the teachers will scratch their heads if asked what good has come from the inspection. A report is written, which is read by hardly anyone, and life goes back to normal.

Not, however, immediately. In the two weeks following an inspection, there is a dramatic reaction. In most schools, there is mass staff absence, of perhaps as many as half the staff for a day or more during that period. Some will be due to staff who had been ill during the inspection week, but refused to be absent, on the basis that it would let the side down. Some will be due to nervous and physical exhaustion. Staff absence may be interpreted in a variety of ways, but in this case the phenomenon is too widespread to be seen as anything other than a function of the Ofsted experience.

There is also a drop in morale. All that effort, and to what end? There is a flatness which always accompanies the end of some prolonged effort. Again, classroom performance flattens, the learning process is in neutral for a while.

There is also the nervous period before the publication of the report. It is true that the Registered Inspector gives an oral report to the headteacher at the end of the inspection. It is also true that it is far from unknown for the written report to differ substantially from the oral report. Staff are naturally anxious about the written word, and whether they can be identified from it.

The last phase follows the publication. Within 40 days, the governors are required to devise an action plan in response to the report. Since the report contains 'Key Points for Action', it might be thought simple enough to copy them out and send them back, but apparently that is considered insufficient. Of course, the governing body is in reality quite incapable of devising an action plan. Like everything else it apparently does, it has to be told by the headteacher. The headteacher will no doubt involve a range of senior staff in the task; or, to put it another way, teachers will be undertaking just one more piece of useless work, writing words which no-one will read, and which will have no effect on the quality of teaching and learning. However, when that is done, that is the end of Ofsted.

Who are the inspectors?

Who are the inspectors who implement this reign of terror? Are they the kind of torturers who, as soon as Ofsted is overthrown, will be charged with inspection crimes? Far from it. The important fact, which undermines all the claims from the government about the Ofsted database, is that the inspectors are a very mixed bunch indeed.

First of all, let us deal with the lay inspector. Somebody who really did believe that a profession is a conspiracy against the laity had inserted into the legislation the requirement that every Ofsted team should have one member whose qualification was that they knew absolutely nothing about schools or teaching. All teachers see this as self-evidently ludicrous, and I have never heard a convincing argument in favour. However, as things have turned out, this provision has not in general been damaging.

In the first place, lay inspectors seem to realise the incongruity of their position, and keep quiet. They can be given lots of useful jobs during the inspection, like checking whether the toilets are kept clean.

Secondly, the logical impossibility of their position has been confirmed by experience: that is to say, after they have taken part in a number of inspections, the lay inspectors no longer know nothing of schools, and some are able to use their experience more constructively.

Lastly, some lay inspectors do have the skills to ask sensible questions about some aspects of the school outside the classrooms. Most typically, they will be able to make worthwhile observations about management issues, such as the relationships between governors, headteacher, senior management, and the staff as a whole. However, all this adds up only to a general absence of harm. Lay inspectors just cannot punch their weight on an inspection team, and should be abolished.

The remainder of inspection teams are professionals. Until recently, most were local authority inspectors. The qualifications for these posts include a wide experience of a particular phase of education, a deep knowledge of the content and pedagogy of a curriculum area and of current educational research, an ability to relate to other professionals, and judgement. It is a rare person who combines these qualities. In some places, these people have been called advisers.

Traditionally, their role has been focused on the classroom, and the quality of teaching. The idea was that the inspector would watch you teach, then spend a considerable amount of time with you explaining what you had done right, what you had done wrong, and giving you detailed advice about how to improve, and perhaps about training opportunities and even your career plans. Then the inspector would put it in writing, and send a copy to your head.

If you were lucky, you received good advice, and your practice improved. If you were unlucky, the advice was useless. In any event, if you were inter-ested in advancing your career in that authority, you paid good attention, since your inspector's opinion would be sought by any appointment committee. By that means, inspectors influenced the style of teaching and learning in their authority. More senior inspectors would work in the same way with headteachers, advising about general school policies.

Two recent developments have affected the work of inspectorates, both for the worse in terms of the service they can offer teachers. One is the tendency to break up local authorities into smaller units. The abolition of the Inner London Education Authority has been followed by the creation of small unitary authorities across the country. There is a very pronounced disec-onomy of scale within the education service.

Looking at inner London, many senior ILEA inspectors were acknowl-edged national authorities in their curriculum areas; minority subject areas, and all phases, could be covered by expert inspectors; and the ILEA inspec-torate was a powerful engine of curriculum and pedagogical development. On abolition, the boroughs could not afford the same number of posts and, with the odd exception, would not share appointments, with consequent loss of service. Only the major subjects were covered; and there was a serious lack of primary inspectors and those with experience of specific special needs. There is no doubt that this is replicated in more recent local government reorganisations. The government now believes that local authorities can fulfil their function by acting as brokers between schools and independent inspection and advisory services.

The second development affects every part of the country, for the introduction of local management of schools has profoundly affected the work of inspectors. Quite apart from the general pressure of year on year cuts in the education service, the allocation of an ever increasing proportion of the budget to the direct control of schools has reduced the ability of authorities to maintain the local inspectorate. The solution adopted in most places has been to devolve the inspectorate, that is, to allocate the costs of the inspectorate to the schools' budget, and to invite schools to buy each year the service they offer. If they do not buy, the inspectorate will disappear. There is absolutely no doubt that this produces a pressure on inspectors to serve not the teachers, but those responsible for schools' spending decisions, the headteachers. The other pressure producing the same result is the much wider range of responsibilities of headteachers under local management.

Inspectors now advise school management on a whole range of issues, such as budget, personnel matters, and so on, for which they may not be qualified, but for which there is no substitute within the stripped down authority staffing. It is now generally understood, and in some cases explicitly stated, that the role of the local inspectorate is to support school management, rather than classroom teachers.

Teachers have always been used to variable quality within the inspectorate. Many of them were inspiring classroom teachers, the kind with lots and lots of ideas about enthusing children, brilliant communicators; in short, ideal as role models and guides for other teachers. Others, I'm afraid, were people who just ordinary. Perhaps they were good at all the mechanics of planning a lesson, and providing good materials, but did not have that spark which lights up relationships between teacher and learners. These tend to become the kind of inspector whose judgement is not trusted.

It is in the nature of things that some people will be better at their jobs than others, and some school inspectors are better than others. One of the differences, which becomes crucial to my argument, is in their ability to make judgements on the quality of the work of teachers. Some are able to be objective, to observe or discover all the relevant contexts of a lesson, to resist being influenced by the attitude of management to a teacher, and to evaluate the teacher with reliability. It is important to realise that some inspectors are less able to do these things. In an LEA, this is not necessarily too damaging. There will be a shared view about the quality of a local inspector's judgement, based on shared knowledge, and a certain amount of discounting can take place. In short, local inspectors gain a local reputation, through which their work is interpreted.

The requirement that inspectors earn their own living, so to speak, resulting from the devolution of funding to schools, coincided with the new earning opportunity represented by the Ofsted regime. Virtually without exception, local inspectors undertook the (short) training to become Ofsted inspectors, and set about forming teams to bid for contracts to carry out Ofsted inspections. The norm has been for the inspectorate to spend part of their time inspecting schools, generally in an authority other than their own, and part of their time offering services to schools in their own authority. Obviously, one result of this is a reduction in the service available locally.

There are other kinds of Ofsted inspection teams. Some organisations established to gain a share of the inspection market have been able to undercut the local authority teams. Now they undertake the majority of primary inspections. Ofsted was also forced to recruit a large number of primary headteachers as registered inspectors when the shortage of teams with primary experience became acute. Incidentally, even now there are more problems associated with inspection in primary and special schools than in secondary schools, largely because of the lack of inspectors with relevant experience, and because of the effect of a large team of visitors on a small institution.

Can we rely on Ofsted statistics?

If it is accepted, as it would be by all teachers, that the quality of local authority inspection teams is variable, then it follows that the quality of Ofsted teams is variable. Amongst other things, this puts a massive question mark next to some of the government's major claims for it. For the organisation, and particularly the database which is given such status, to have credibility, Ofsted must be able to show that its inspection evidence is both reliable and valid, in the statistical sense. There is substantial evidence that neither is the case.

If its evidence was reliable, replication of inspection of an individual school by a different inspection team would produce the same results, if undertaken within a short space of time. There are sufficient examples of the contrary to show that the degree of reliability is very poor. Most of the examples available are due to the habit of many LEAs of conducting mock inspections shortly before the real thing. The authority's own inspectors, who are of course Ofsted inspectors, go through the Ofsted routine, with the aim of helping the school to present itself positively for the real inspection.

It might be argued that if a school receives a better report the second time, the LEAs aim has been achieved. Unfortunately, things do not work like that. The results of the two are habitually very different, and a worse judgement by the Ofsted team is as common as the opposite. Particularly noticeable are the many examples of schools which have been regarded as satisfactory by their own authority, only to be labelled 'failing' by the subsequent Ofsted inspection. It is not my case that either the local authority or the Ofsted team has the superior judgement; it is my case that since both are, in effect, Ofsted teams, there is no consistency of judgement.

Even more interesting evidence is provided by those cases in which Ofsted disagrees with itself. We have for example the case of a London secondary school which was found to be failing. The staff, governors and parents were incensed, because they all had a different view, and waged a considerable campaign. When the HMI visited, as is required by the system, it decided that the school was not failing. But, for some reason, Her Majesty's Government's Chief Inspector decided the school was to be under special measures. So, it becomes another failing school statistic.

Another type of evidence, though perhaps slightly less conclusive, is from teachers who have the bad luck to be inspected twice by virtue of changing their jobs. Incidentally, schools now routinely include in advertisements for staff the information that 'the school received an excellent Ofsted report recently'. Some readers might assume the school is trying to convince potential applicants of the worth of the school. The real reason, however, is to encourage applicants by pointing out that they will not have to face 'the big O' for a long time. Headteachers, in particular, have often tried to keep one jump ahead of Ofsted by leaving a school which faces one for a school which has had one, and many other astute teachers plan career moves with the same thing in mind.

However, many teachers cannot plan their careers with only that consideration, and consequently there are many who have been inspected, have moved to a different school, and been inspected again. Naturally, there are no statistics on this, but it seems it is very common for the assessments made in these circumstances to vary widely. Teachers believe that this evidence confirms the unreliability of the judgements made by Ofsted inspectors.

From a more theoretical point of view, also, the lack of reliability is to be expected. The most controversial items in the Ofsted databank are, in fact, accumulations not of fact but of judgement. We can have a fascinating and unresolvable argument about the significance of 10%, 50% or 90% of pupils attaining 5 GCSEs at A-C, but at least it is a fact. Whether 50%, 75% or 100% of lessons are taught satisfactorily or better is not a fact at all. It's not even a judgement. It is actually a large number of judgements.

This is not the place to rehearse the discussion around the proposition that there is not even consensus about what constitutes satisfactory teaching in any given situation — but that is surely true. In addition to that major problem, there is the phenomenon that two observers witnessing an event observe very different things, and in a social situation as complex as a classroom, where there are thousands of individual interactions between teacher and pupils each day, we would expect this phenomenon to be prominent.

Every lesson seen by an inspector is graded. Until recently, there were 7 grades, but because inspectors were unable to find sufficient lessons to fit the bottom two grades, there are now 3 grades. There was an elaborate procedure surrounding the award of the grades 1 and 2, and 6 and 7, which probably explains why inspectors were reluctant to use them.

The question to be asked, however, is what, if anything, these grades mean? The grade descriptors were laughable in terms of operationalising a differentiation. These have now been replaced by the labels 'Good', 'Satisfactory' and 'Poor'. Whatever the grading system, but particularly with a small number of grades, there is no difficulty in placing a large number of people in one or the other.

The problem is at the grade boundaries, where there is an even larger number of people. No matter how much honest people wrestle with the problem, there is no way of devising grade descriptors which are capable of producing unambiguous allocations of individual teachers to grades, whether there are three or seven. Teaching is just too complex an activity, and reliant on just too many external factors.

I have already argued that there is a very poor level of reliability in inspectors' assessments of performance. It is at the moment when those subjective and unreliable judgements become translated into numbers that the intellectual fraud is committed, for then the judgements are given objective status. The numbers become facts. They can be added, extrapolated, and averaged. Statistically gothic creations are devised from the database. x% satisfactory lessons at Key Stage 1 — it's a fact. Only y% satisfactory lessons at Key Stage 2 — that's a fact, as well. 88 teachers out of ten thousand graded 6 or 7 — oh no, that's not a fact, that's a mistake. It is all nonsense.

If there is a lack of reliability in the information gained from Ofsted inspections, is it valid? Valid information might be described as having a close correspondence to reality. Those items which are judgements clearly are not open to a test of validity. More depressing is the number of factual errors which appear in Ofsted reports, and hence in the database. There is an obvious connection with the issue of lack of responsiveness discussed above. In other words, not only can you not trust the judgements in an Ofsted report, but you cannot believe the information in it either.

The problems I describe have been experienced by teachers who feel very strongly about errors of judgement and fact when the standards expected of them are so high. However, my contentions are not based only on anecdotal evidence. There is substantial research, by pressure groups such as Article 26, by academics and particularly by Ofsted itself, which casts doubt on the quality of the database. Problems of inconsistency of judgement and of operating grade boundaries are significant and continuing.

No doubt some readers will be muttering words about obscure philosophical arguments far removed from the real need to measure and improve school performance. Unfortunately, the resulting policies will fail precisely because they are intellectually fraudulent. Ofsted will start to make progress when it deletes all the items in the database which are not based on data, and stops using it to generate slogans.

Professional accountability?

There is one last argument, put by the proponents of this juggernaut, which requires some attention. It is that the nation's schools consume a huge amount of public funds, and therefore schools and teachers must be accountable. Ofsted is the mechanism by which the state, representing the people, brings schools to account.

It is true that the accountability of some professionals leaves something to be desired. I understand that pursuing a solicitor who has been negligent with your affairs is not an easy matter, for example. I cannot believe that the majority of this country's citizens see the accountability of teachers as a problem.

First of all, I say with all conviction that there is a very high degree of self-accountability amongst teachers. Teachers are not in the business for money. They have what can only be described as a vocation. They put up with everything because they want to serve. There are exceptions, of course, but most teachers set high standards of themselves — too high, quite often — and feel it more than anyone else if they let themselves down.

Second, there is the accountability of the staff room. There is a strong culture of teaching, and one of its values is what is often called collegiality. Teachers have high illness levels and low sickness absence levels, because they do not want to let down their colleagues. Teachers want to pull their weight, and there is general disdain in the staff room for those who do not.

I do not expect these arguments to wash with cynics, or those hard politicians who need results, and fast. However, there are two other layers of accountability for teachers which cannot be ignored.

Third, teachers, through their schools, are directly and continuously accountable to the local state, the local education authority. No-one can deny that education issues, including matters concerning individual schools, are the business of local politics, in which the local voter can and does play an active part. My guess is that more ordinary people become active in local campaigns about schools than any other political issue. People still do not understand or accept that the present system of local management has largely created the situation that he who pays the piper does not call the tune, but I am sure that the illogicality of present arrangements will be put right eventually.

Fourth, and most importantly, teachers are in practice increasingly accountable in the way that really matters: for older pupils, to the pupils themselves, and for all pupils, to their parents and carers. MPs are said to be accountable once every five years, but no doubt it could be argued they face their public every fortnight at their surgeries. Primary teachers face their public every afternoon, and perhaps every morning as well. You can bet that the parent who is unhappy about something in her child's classroom will take an early opportunity to appraise the teacher of her views. Your average parent would not take kindly to 'I've noted your point. I'll reply in writing within a month.' Your average parent wants action now. Deal with the class bully. Give more/less homework. Make the child work harder. Why doesn't the child know his tables? *That* is accountability. The mechanisms change in secondary schools. Very often, the pupil applies the pressure. *That* is accountability. And it is not only middle class parents who give the school a hard time about a teacher they perceive as incompetent.

The truth is, teachers are accountable, and in a number of ways to a number of constituencies. The profession is unusual in being immediately and continuously exposed to the responses of those to whom they are giving service. The truth is, when the government says it wants accountability, it means it wants schools to be accountable to it — and for accountability, read control. The immense and rapid centralisation of power over schools in recent years has been well documented.

I believe schools are best administered locally, and I think most people in this country agree. As long as people can enter their child's school and get things done, as long as they can lobby their councillor, demonstrate outside the town hall, and get things done, the schools of this country will remain accountable in the ways that matter.

This is not palatable to a new government which is committed to change in schools, but it will have to learn that the only way to achieve change is through a partnership which is real and not a slogan. In its efforts to by-pass the local, the government has used Ofsted as the state's secret police for the education service. Ofsted is failing to produce any improvement in standards. If it is to make any contribution to the crusade, the inspection regime and the inspection machine should be radically revised.

Definitions of failure

Now let us examine how Ofsted inspections actually work, as far as teachers in schools for the underclass are concerned.

The Ofsted position seems to be that the categories 'inner city sink school' and 'failing school' are distinct and unconnected. The fact is that there is a very substantial overlap between the two. Not only is a substantial proportion of such schools failed by Ofsted, but a substantial proportion of failed schools serve the underclass. There is another group of schools, special schools for emotionally and behaviourally disturbed pupils, with a high failure rate; but that is another story.

Ofsted makes great play of the fact that all kinds of schools are found to be failures, including small village schools and apparently respectable but underachieving schools. However, my analysis of the secondary schools deemed to require special measures up to May 1997 suggests that at least 70% of them had exceptionally difficult intakes. This figure alone casts huge doubt on what might be described as efforts to socially decontextualise school performance. Later research reinforces this view.

Ofsted's 'Framework for the Inspection of Schools' lays down the criteria for judging that a school is failing.

(1) *the management and efficiency of the school*, including the ineffectiveness of the headteacher, senior management or governors; loss of confidence in the headteacher; demoralisation amongst the staff; poor management of resources and poor value for money.

(2) *the quality of education provided*. This includes a high proportion of unsatisfactory teaching; failure to implement the National Curriculum; poor provision for pupils' spiritual, moral, social and cultural development; pupils at physical or emotional risk from other pupils or adults; 'abrasive and confrontational relationships' between staff and pupils.

The judgement should be based on the extent to which some or all of the characteristics listed are evident. Clearly, none of them on its own is likely to be sufficient. Some might suggest that some of them are universal features of our schools at the moment — the teacher unions, for example, would point to demoralisation of staff. Others would argue that almost all governing bodies are very largely ineffective in practice.

One concern is the extent to which these characteristics are within the control of the staff. An obvious example is the question of relationships between staff and pupils. To put it simply, it takes two to tango. It is just not the case that pupils are passive recipients of a style of relationship. Indeed, I have argued that the oppositional stance of children of the underclass is a very significant determinant of everything that happens in their schools.

This question becomes salient when considering the third set of criteria for judging whether a school is failing.

(3) *the educational standards achieved.* These include: low attainment by the majority of pupils; regular disruptive behaviour, breakdown of discipline; significant levels of racial tension or harassment; poor attendance by a substantial proportion of pupils. On the face of it, these are perfectly reasonable criteria for judging a school. But are they reasonable criteria for judging its staff?

It is important to bear in mind that there is another criterion, the quality of education provided, which deals with the quality of the job being done by teachers in the classroom. It is actually far from unknown for a school to be judged failing even though the quality of the teaching is generally sound, as they say.

It is difficult to escape the conclusion that the standards criterion judges the performance not of the staff, but of the pupils, and I hope I do not have to prolong the argument to assert that there is a difference between the two. A recent incident illustrates the point. A colleague who is a head of department in an inner London secondary school suffered an inspection by a team from one of the organisations which win a very large number of Ofsted contracts. At the end of the week, an inspector told my colleague that a member of the department was to be graded 1 (i.e. was judged to be an outstanding teacher), and went on to say that in his experience teachers in London were never graded 1, because their pupils' academic performance did not merit it. We may all conclude that, under the present regime, ambitious teachers should never work in the inner city because they will be judged on their results, which can never be as good in raw terms as those obtained in the suburbs.

An example at the other end of the scale provides further illustration. A school in Greater Manchester was reported by Ofsted inspectors to be excellent. Yet when Her Majesty's Chief Inspector produced a list of excellent schools, this one failed to appear. Investigation by an unhappy headteacher revealed that the school failed to meet one of the excellence criteria: its GCSE results were not good enough. Ofsted had failed to take into account the fact that the school was a secondary modern in a selective system, so that it was planned not to have excellent GCSE results, in terms of raw scores.

The other items in this criterion are equally largely dependent on the pupil intake. Racial tension, for example, is so obviously generated outside the school that to judge a school on its presence amounts to perversity. The propensities of pupils to truant, or to be present but disruptive, are also external to the school.

How can it make sense to judge one school to be better than another because it has never had to face these problems to any significant extent? How can it make sense to judge the other worse, because these issues are endemic in the intake, and only partially solved as pupils move through the school? Naturally, a school should be found at fault if it makes no effort to address truancy, racism, or disruption — but I don't think I've ever found one which did not struggle against them. Neither should a school be excused for complacency about only partial success; but the theme of this book is that these phenomena are embedded deep in our society, are perennial, and resist eradication in all our institutions. Teachers do not enjoy working in such atmospheres; indeed, such conditions are literally killing. No wonder they feel deeply angry and depressed when pilloried for not finding all the answers despite their best efforts.

The school makes a difference. Of course it does. No-one is suggesting that the items considered in the educational standards criterion are not affected by the staff performance. To re-iterate, however, the way the staff tackle them is judged elsewhere in the criteria. This double jeopardy is not only a major weakness of the criteria, but the major reason why there is such a close correspondence between the categories of 'school for the underclass' and 'failing school'.

Inspection in the underclass school

What kind of experience is Ofsted week for teachers in the underclass school? They have spent a long time preparing a week's show lessons. They are not realistic lessons, because far more preparation has gone into them than can ever be managed on a regular basis.

In some other schools, the classes will not be realistic either. Some headteachers go to great lengths to ensure that some of the most disruptive pupils do not darken the door of the school during the inspection. They may be informally excluded, on the apparent grounds that a place in some special unit is being investigated. They may simply be encouraged to be absent. This is not an option in the underclass school. Potential disruption is endemic, not sporadic, and cannot be screened out.

There is also the Ofsted effect on the pupils. Any visitor to a classroom will have an effect on the class dynamics. This is a complex matter, determined by the type of pupil, the behaviour of the visitor, the relationship between the visitor and the teacher, and so on. Pupils have a variety of reactions to inspectors. Many of them take on the role of teacher support. They approach teachers who are walking down a corridor: 'Watch out, miss, there's an inspector round the corner.' Those who feel positive about their teachers will act like co-performers in the classroom. The result is a show lesson, with show pupils taking part. Last week and next week, they are just not bothered, but this week, the hands go up, the pens speed across the paper, they are as bright as buttons.

In schools where most pupils do not feel positive about their teachers, however, the teachers are under great stress all week. Last week and next week, the pupils make life a misery. Will they do the same this week? In some cases, unfortunately, the disruption is compounded. Perhaps it is an example of any visitor, or change of routine, being hard to cope with, as is the case with many disturbed youngsters; perhaps it is a deliberate act, aimed at influencing an inspector's judgement.

However, the realities will break through at times in the week. There will be the usual defiance, outbursts, disturbances. Teachers already sweating because the inspector is sitting at the back of the room will suffer stress overload when the usual suspects play up. The proportion of pupils who do their homework will not magically rise for this week, and the exercise books will not lie. As I have explained, the inspector is not only judging the quality of the lesson as taught, but also the quality of the reactions of the learners — or non-learners.

Sooner or later, an inspector calls. Perhaps the inspectors accompany the teachers to the start of the lesson, perhaps they drop in after it has started. Perhaps they leave before the end, or perhaps they stay to watch the finale. Seldom will the whole lesson be seen, and very often only a few minutes, perhaps fifteen or twenty.

The very short time that is spent seeing each teacher is one major complaint, and one major reason why so many judgements by inspectors are unreliable. Any teacher knows that a lesson is like a story: it has a beginning, a middle, and an end, and is incomplete without all its parts. As public speakers are always taught, first you tell 'em what you're going to say, then you say it, then you tell 'em what you've said. It is difficult enough to evaluate a lesson without knowing the contexts of both the scheme of work of which it is a part, and also the nature of the group being taught.

In primary schools, the problem is different. The large primary school has half the staff of the small secondary school. Many primary schools have 10 teachers or fewer. The Ofsted team all but swamps a primary school. Each teacher is likely to be seen repeatedly, as individual components of the national curriculum are assessed separately for each Key Stage. Strangely, the problem of short visits is often repeated, so that the teachers suffer a series of observations, each too short to provide a realistic view of the whole session. Unlike secondary staff, primary teachers may feel under siege, knowing that they are to be visited frequently, without knowing when, and knowing that the inspector is unlikely to be able to understand what is going on because of the brevity of the visits. Teachers believe it to be impossible to evaluate a lesson without seeing all of it.

The teachers have another complaint. The inspector drops in, and goes away. That is the end of it, as far as the individual teacher is concerned. I have already pointed out that it is a considerable waste of a valuable resource that the teacher is given virtually no feedback afterwards. How else can teachers reflect on their practice, try new ideas, improve their performance? Following complaints about this, feedback is now a requirement, but rarely amounts to anything more than a very general comment on the lessons observed.

But a debrief of a lesson would have another advantage. In such a discussion, the inspector would become more aware of the teacher's strengths and weaknesses, but would also learn more about the lesson; its rationale, its contexts, the particularities of the group taught, and so on. The Ofsted team's understanding of the school and its pupils would be greatly enhanced by such a process.

If Ofsted claims that the answer to the problems of the underclass school is better teaching, is it not reasonable to expect the Ofsted inspectors to explain how to teach better? Of course, in practice they do not have the answers any more than the people they are inspecting, but as long as they pretend otherwise, that should be the requirement.

It is the headteacher of the to-be-failed school who has the worst of it. The headteacher will have sessions with the leader of the inspection team before, every day during, and at the end of, the inspection, to discuss the inspection itself, and to receive feedback. The head will be warned during the week that the school is in danger of failing.

The smart ones then jump through hoops to avert the disaster. Too many weak lessons in Key Stage 3 core subjects? Fix some show lessons with the strongest staff and the best classes, and make sure the inspectors see them. Too disorderly in the public places? Bring in or redeploy extra staff, blitz the corridors, and ask the inspectors to look again. In some cases, this has actually worked, but the head needs a very sympathetic inspection team.

More often than not, however, the panic measures do not work. The school is seen for what it is, warts and all, or just warts. At the end of the week, the headteacher has the melancholy task of receiving confirmation of sentence from the inspectors, and of passing on the message to the staff.

I am a classroom teacher. I have very little idea what transpires at that final debriefing session. I believe that it often enables the headteacher to take part in a certain amount of haggling about the team's conclusions, where they are based on misconceived observation.

One thing I know about life, however, is that where there is an opportunity for miscommunication, miscommunication will occur. Experience shows that strange misunderstandings develop between the Registered Inspector's oral report to the head, the head's subsequent reports to staff, and the final written report. Bearing in mind that the headteacher is more in the firing line than any other member of staff, perhaps this is not surprising. However, this is an important example of the ways that almost everything reported to classroom teachers by the inspectors is mediated through others, mainly their managers.

Oh, and there is very often a third task for the head: to fill a briefcase with the mug, the family pictures from the desk, and the tablets, before slipping quietly away, never to return.

In the failing school

After the inspection, there is a period of suspended animation. HMI must visit, to confirm the inspectors' verdict. Then there is the wait for the written report.

When it arrives, the usual reaction from the staff is of anger. There is intense discussion about all the detailed mistakes of fact, or judgement, and all the misunderstandings. Most of all, the anger is against inspectors who appear not to have noticed the problems posed by the pupils, whose expectations appear quite unrealistic, whose experience and understanding of the underclass appears completely lacking. The frustration is heightened by the lack of anyone to argue with. The Registered Inspector will never be seen again.

The local authority is forced to appear shocked, concerned, dynamic, and productive. It can be very supportive, but is often just an annoyance, as it fusses around without having the slightest idea what to do. If it removes delegated powers, as some authorities tend to do, it may well find that it has insufficient staff to undertake the monitoring and strategic role supposedly undertaken by the governors.

In many cases, its first task is to decide whether the headteacher is part of the problem or part of the solution, unless the decision has already been taken. I believe that under local management, it is extremely difficult for an authority to make that judgement. Being at arm's length from the school, it has had to rely for information about the school from — the head. The only people with close knowledge of the head's performance are likely to be the school's inspector, and the chair of governors. The latter is hardly likely to have any basis for judgement. The former has had the duty to see the school from the management's perspective.

You may be sure that one group which will have no say in the matter is the teaching staff. The normal state of affairs is that it takes industrial action by teachers to move an authority to listen to their frustrations about their management.

If the headteacher gets the thumbs down, the next big headache for the authority is: who is going to run the school? Who can take charge for the time being, while a permanent appointment is sought? And who, apart from a completely deranged masochist, would want the job? I shall return to this matter, which concerns a number of Chief Education Officers, especially in London, but it should be said here that in a number of cases, that particular problem is never resolved satisfactorily.

However, it is the local authority inspectorate which has the dominant role in turning the school round, as they say. As explained elsewhere, the problem here is that the inspectorate is financially free-standing, and must sell its services to schools. In the months to come, the inspectors will swarm all over the school, and the bill will run into tens of thousands of pounds. Unless the authority does a deal, the financial crisis that accompanies special measures status is thereby considerably exacerbated.

The first task is to complete the Action Plan, which takes on a far greater significance than in schools which have passed. Quantified targets are the subject of discussion between school and authority, and between school and HMI. Each failing school will have its particularities, but a consistent theme is the requirement to increase the percentage of lessons where the teaching and learning is judged satisfactory or better. The target for this will be expressed exactly, but the means of achieving it will be stated in very general terms.

Often, much of the plan will focus on aspects of bureaucracy. There is a simple reason for this. The production and implementation of new policies and procedures, normally involving paperwork, is comparatively easy to execute and monitor. A whole-school policy for marking, say? Work it out, tick it off, impress the HMI, another step on the road to recovery. A list of such tasks in the Action Plan gives the impression of — action.

Only at this time, the half-term in which the Action Plan is being drawn up, does the staff as a whole start to understand the position it is in. However much it was expected, being placed in special measures is a shock, a slap in the face, an official statement that each of those teachers who have been swimming in a freezing sea against a tide of overwhelming waves is useless, style all wrong, not fit enough, or whatever, but just not good enough to make any headway. After a pause, morale sinks like a stone. At the same time, the pressure starts to be applied. In secondary schools, only the senior staff will be involved in writing the Action Plan, with the inspector.

As its contents become known, staff unease mounts. The teachers thought that the intolerable pressure of work in the period before the Ofsted inspection was a one-off. Only now do they begin to see that the intolerable is going to have to be tolerated indefinitely. Perhaps after a pause while the Action Plan is being approved by HMI, the treadmill starts again.

There will be staff meetings about, say, the new whole-school marking policy. Interminable meetings to discuss the principles and details; everyone has to take part, even though they think the management has already decided what is going to happen, and the consultation is a sham. Further meetings to announce the decisions, and train the staff to implement the new policy. And the punch-line, the arrangements for staff to submit on a regular basis a sample of books so that the implementation can be checked.

Schools in special measures are not given the luxury of a one-step-at-a-time approach. Everything must be done at once. On the headteacher's calendar, there is a large circle around the date of the HMI's next visit. The staff may be more or less aware of that date, but you may be assured it is soon, and we must show progress in every aspect of the Action Plan then.

So, yes, we can tick off the marking policy, oh, and by the way there'll be a formal disciplinary warning for Ms Smith, for not fully following it; she has to understand the pressures we're all under, being off for four weeks with stress is no excuse for not catching up when she came back. As well as the marking policy, the school is developing new procedures on this and that; all of them will require similar time-consuming meetings, and time-consuming adaptation by all the teachers of their own practice. As well as all those procedures, the department is under the cosh about improving its results. As well as all that, the pupils are as they were — recalcitrant, demotivated, difficult to handle, and stress-creating.

Imagine yet another meeting, this time the weekly departmental meeting. The head of department reports the results of the monitoring of marking, then disseminates the new guidelines on releasing pupils from lessons, which replace the guidelines imposed during the run-up to Ofsted — both seem unworkable to most staff present. Then on to departmental results.

'Our inspection report says the Key Stage 3 scheme of work is no good, so we've got to produce a new one quickly.'

'Hang on,' replies the resident Bolshie, 'we sweated blood over that scheme of work only two terms ago.'

'I know, but Ofsted said it did not meet the National Curriculum. Anyway, the boss says we've got to do it, so there it is.'

'But Caligula [pet name for the local authority subject inspector] told us it was fine, just the job for the inspection. How are we meant to know what we're supposed to do?'

'Look, don't be difficult. Let's just get on with it. I had a chat with Caligula when she was in last week. She was a bit miffed that we had misunderstood her advice, but she's — '

'We what?! She told us quite clearly what she wanted, we did — '

'There's no point in going on, the scheme of work is not what the HMI want, we've got to do a new one, and Caligula will be in next Tuesday to take us through it. Sorry it's short notice for an extra meeting, but that's the only time she could make it.'

To the disbelieving reader, I am forced to insist that this scenario is far from uncommon. A frequent complaint from teachers in schools under special measures is that they receive conflicting advice or instruction from different sources, with the local inspectorate and the HMI often the sources. In other words, the staff bust a gut to implement a new procedure as recommended, only for it to be rejected when HMI visit to check progress.

Since the staff suspended their professional judgement in doing what they were told in the first place, this whole process only increases the feelings of deprofessionalisation, of alienation, of becoming a cog in a very impersonal machine. If staff morale sinks like a stone during the Action Plan period, as the special measures process grinds on, term after term, it sinks even lower.

But back to the departmental meeting, for it will have other business. A dozen schemes for squeezing higher standards from the pupils will be discussed. Each of them will involve extra work, extra records, extra monitoring. A key requirement will be the recording and monitoring of lesson plans. What for teachers in other schools is a time-wasting and irksome task in the pre-Ofsted period becomes a permanent feature of life here.

Quality experienced professionals, who know their subject, know their pupils, know what works, and teach well, have their professionalism implicitly questioned, have their spontaneity removed, and are forced to record in minute detail and in standard form every thing they do. It is demeaning, but worse, it is time-consuming, it reduces the time available for more useful work. It is pointless bureaucracy. This requirement, along with the checking of these records by management and inspectors, creates the atmosphere of control and surveillance of staff in a failing school which is immediately recognisable and quite intolerable.

It is necessary to remember, here, that the very large majority of the teachers in the school have never had their competence questioned, either by Ofsted or anyone else. No-one is suggesting they are not sound teachers. Yet individually and collectively, special measures places them under a pressure which is both stressful almost beyond endurance and counter-productive.

The special measures process is counter-productive because the work and stress are seldom directed in the areas of school life which matter. It does not address the fundamental questions about the performance of the pupils. In the view of virtually all staff, the issue which needs addressing is the management of the behaviour of pupils, both in classrooms and around the school. This is one topic which is avoided. If raised by staff, the typical answer is that the various schemes will indirectly improve behaviour, because the quality of teaching will improve. This goes down like a lead balloon.

It is not always like that, and does not have to be. Some failing schools bring in inspectors or consultants to advise and train staff in individual and whole staff techniques and policies for dealing with difficult behaviour, but they are a minority.

Another problem commonly avoided is the way the staff are directed and led by the management. Whether the head was in post pre-Ofsted, or is an acting or permanent replacement, the pressure of special measures often finds them out. There is a clear connection between these two issues, the management of pupil behaviour and the quality of leadership. As I show elsewhere, few headteachers these days have the skills and willingness to show leadership in dealing with difficult behaviour. 'The kids are rioting outside, but the boss hides herself under a pile of paper in her office,' is a comment I have heard often. (In case you are wondering, the speaker does not mean the word 'riot' to be taken in a completely literal sense. That does remain an unusual event.) Unfortunately, if they are not leaders, often neither are they managers with sufficient skills to help the organisation through such a difficult situation, although it must be recognised that the level of skill required is very high indeed.

So, week in and week out, the teachers in the special measures school face the multiple horrors of disruption in the classroom, endless hours of meaningless paperwork, saturation surveillance by senior staff, local inspectors and the occasional HMI visit, all within an atmosphere of general uncertainty about the future. The rumour factory works overtime, and school closure is always a possibility; it is far from unknown for the threat of closure to be used as a stick by management.

Injury on insult

In the middle of all this, another rumour starts, and quickly becomes reality: the school will suffer redundancies. The reasons for this are simple. As explained earlier, the current admissions arrangements have the effect of speeding the movement of schools up and down the popularity hierarchy. The school for the underclass, typically, will have reduced the number of pupils on roll before the Ofsted inspection. Each year, the number transferring from primary schools is lower than the number leaving at age 16. Under the local management of schools, at least 75% of the resources available to a school must be on the basis of pupil numbers, so that each year since the introduction of local management most schools for the underclass have had a budget reduction. In most cases, the amounts are manageable. Given the typical teacher turnover in such schools, it is relatively easy to reduce staffing by non-replacement of leavers.

However, the Ofsted failure normally provokes a financial crisis. Firstly, the rate of loss of pupils tends to increase. It would not be true to say that there is a wholesale flight; after all, pupil and parent experience of the school does not significantly change; but the failure does trigger some additional movement, and hence a further budget reduction. Secondly, however, it places the budget, like all other aspects of the school, under a spotlight.

It is a matter of record that the spotlight frequently reveals astonishing financial mismanagement. Given that both income and expenditure in a school are relatively easy to predict, the accumulation of deficits exceeding 10% of budget without correcting action is irresponsible, but the rule rather than the exception in failing schools.

Of course, there is another way to look at it: if the resources available to these schools are inadequate, headteachers could be justified in maintaining necessary levels of provision regardless of the budget position, but only if the position can be sustained on a long-term basis. It cannot. Sooner or later, the school will be required to bring the budget back to balance. I am bound to report that the budget deficit found in most failing schools is not due to principled defiance, but plain mismanagement. The result is that, some time after special measures are imposed, the staff will be told that the school has a £150,000 (£250,000, £350,000) deficit, it will get worse next year, and there have to be redundancies.

It is hard to imagine the effect of such an announcement. As far as staff are concerned, although individually they have done nothing wrong, nor been incompetent, their school has been put through the mangle, given a very public rejection, and they have co-operated in making their own lives a misery by complying with every demand made of them, only to be told they are unwanted.

It is a hammer blow. In the event, there is usually a period of a few weeks of manoeuvring between management and unions, following which sufficient teachers volunteer to leave to make compulsory redundancy unnecessary, although on occasion it is not quite clear whether the volunteer jumped or was pushed. That period, however, is immensely damaging to the school. The sense of rejection, of another unjust punishment, crushes forever the commitment to the school which has sustained the staff through thin and thin.

The staff reductions are a watershed. Afterwards, the staff continue their work, but the coercive powers of management and inspection replace commitment as the motivator of performance. A more cynical tone becomes dominant in the staff room. The other damage, of course, is the effect of the cuts themselves. The same amount of work is done by fewer staff. Already stretched to the limits, the staff will experience larger classes, perhaps fewer non-contact periods, and many will have to learn new responsibilities. This adds a tinge of resentment to the cynicism. The excitement dies down. The school returns to its apparently endless cycle of initiatives, paperwork, stress and surveillance, with the HMI visit peaking each cycle. Somehow, the school is never quite the same.

The role of the HMI in the special measures procedure is simple. Inspectors visit the school periodically to examine whether it continues to fail 'to provide its pupils with an acceptable standard of education.' To re-iterate, it is not the standards of the teachers, but the standards of the pupils, which are being inspected. Targets of pupil performance are set: x% to achieve A-C GCSE, for example. It will be claimed that the standard of teaching is the focus, with targets for the percentage of satisfactory lessons, but the problem remains that satisfactory lessons in the sense meant by the inspectors includes a response from pupils which they may not be inclined to give, regardless of the technical quality of the teaching.

It is important to understand that these visits are inspections. Their purpose is not to offer support or advice to management, much less the classroom teachers, but only to judge. As described above, it is far from uncommon for the inspector to condemn practices implemented with immense effort by the staff on the advice of the local authority inspectorate, or other consultants. What the inspector will not do is to advise how to reach the targets that have been set. If a target is reached, the inspector will make an approving noise and set another target in some other area of the school's work.

Inevitably, tension rises within the school as the date of the HMI visit approaches. Staff have slaved endlessly, despite the frustration that the real issues are not being addressed — but will the results turn out to be what the inspector wants? And what will be the next demand? And will there ever be an end to this nightmare? In moments of frankness, headteachers of failing schools have told me that they are being inspected to death, by a combination of the HMI and the local inspectorate. They recognise that the effect on morale of this constant judging and equally constant lack of real advice and support is immense and damaging.

They dare not say this publicly; after all, it is their performance which is above all under scrutiny. The day of the visit comes and goes. The HMI reports to the headteacher, and the headteacher passes on the messages to the staff. Progress here, more work needed there, this target achieved, that target set. There's light at the end of the tunnel.

How far away is the light? How long does the agony continue? Or, to put it another way, how long does it take to turn round a failing school? For that group of schools which were failing only because of inadequate management, there is an answer. The appointment of a decent headteacher, and the establishment of good routines, can restore normality within a couple of years.

However, since the bulk of failing secondary schools are schools for the underclass, and there is no such easy answer. Of the 641 schools judged to be failing up to June 1998, just 110, or 17%, had subsequently been found sufficiently improved to be taken off the list. 83% of schools failed by Ofsted since 1993 remained in special measures in June 1998, or had been closed. For many of these schools, the situation seems like permanent revolution. There is no prospect of peace. There is no word of armistice. The light at the end of the tunnel gets no nearer. MPs have been known to ask questions in the House about when the punishment might end for schools in their constituencies, but have been told nothing.

Now the government's policy is more unyielding. The Secretary of State has powers to close a school after two years in special measures. We may presume that closure is an option considered at the time a school fails, and the reasons for rejecting it are always simply practical. It may be that closure would lead to a shortage of school places locally. Our experience is that the school for the underclass cannot be 'turned round' in a short time, because its problems are long-standing and deep-seated.

Some schools for the underclass have passed an Ofsted inspection. I believe the usual reason for this is that the Registered Inspector has, as one might say, a 'sympathetic understanding' of the problems faced by the school. My understanding is that some of those have been 'found out' by the internal monitoring processes of Ofsted, and subsequently win no further inspection contracts. The fact is that those schools will not escape forever. As long as the present inspection regime lasts, every school for the underclass can be confident that it will be caught. Does it not produce exam results far below national averages? Very well, then, it is failing. Under the new system of targeting, the school will be picked off.

Let me sum up. Ofsted is an organisation established for political purposes. Whatever the purposes of school inspections, they could be fulfilled more effectively by other means. It plays absolutely no direct part in improving school performance, because its role is to inspect rather than to advise. Its much vaunted database is a fraud. It should be abolished in its present form, but of course it is too much of a political totem.

Local authorities should be given the resources to operate effective teams combining inspection and advice; these should be monitored by an independent national inspectorate. Inspections should be without notice. There should be an end to the standard report format, with qualitative rather than quantitative assessments and substantive suggestions for development. The government has taken a step in the right direction by its decision to replace the present system with 'light-touch' inspections for most schools, and to target schools which are cause for concern, but it needs to go further. It must end what amounts to victimisation of underclass schools. It must institute support for these schools and the communities they serve, rather than castigating them for failing to achieve impossible targets.

My considered opinion is that working life in Ofsted failing schools is a living hell. Nobody should be required to put up with the hour upon hour of useless work, the immense stresses of being inspected to death on top of the immense strains of doing the job in the classroom, the complete lack of real support, and all misdirected and unproductive in terms of the life chances of the school's pupils.

The teacher unions have utterly failed to protect their members from this inhumane treatment, and the teachers themselves are just too exhausted and demoralised to organise resistance for themselves. I am angry at a society which first excludes millions of people, and then hounds those whose vocation is to support the excluded ones. At the moment, very many of these heroes are being driven to breakdowns. Above all, it is these broken people who have driven me to write this book, and tell this truth.

6

EXCELLENCE IN SCHOOLS?

W HAT IS AN EXCELLENT SCHOOL? The White Paper, *Excellence in Schools*, made it completely clear. Away with those boring philosophical arguments! Away with those who are not on the can-do trip! It is quite simple. An excellent secondary school is one in which the highest possible percentage of pupils attains at least five GCSEs at Grade C or above. We know that there are some truly excellent schools in the country already. They achieve 100%. Only hopelessly negative people would suggest that these schools select their intake on the basis that they are the most able, so that a score of less than 100% should indicate that the school is failing.

The can-do school

We know also that, for the others, the government has set realistic but ambitious targets for the year 2002. It recognises that some schools have further to go. All through this book, I have been showing myself up as old-fashioned by use of the title, 'school for the underclass'. I should have called them the further-to-go schools. In the further-to-go school, the teachers are to increase radically the magic percentage from the current 5%-15%, which is typical of the schools discussed here.

What rejoicing there will be in the staffrooms of the further-to-go schools in 2002 when all those illiterates who entered the school in 1997 proudly collect their GCSE certificates! Their elder sisters and brothers all will have hated school and will have left with nothing as soon as they could, but these will have turned out so differently! What will have made the difference? Let us look at the government's ideas for the necessary transformation of the further-to-go school. All these initiatives have to be judged against their effectiveness in removing the inhibitions on achievement which currently affect performance in some schools, but not all.

Government rhetoric on achievement has not only continued but intensified since the 1997 election, to the intense disappointment of most teachers. The repeated protestation 'background no excuse' severely limits the ability of government to make a realistic analysis or to take effective action. It is also very outdated. Of course it was necessary to move on from the rhetoric of the sixties and seventies that social background was the only significant determinant of achievement, but in truth the school improvement movement was creating that change of thinking long before governments sloganised it. Schools have long understood that what they do can make a difference.

It is difficult to know, however, what difference these intellectual arguments make to the actual performance of teachers in classrooms. Those staffroom debates which stimulated my Friday thirst as a young teacher took for granted that the vast majority of our pupils would be educational failures; the questions were what we could do to make a difference which we all knew would be tiny, and what others could do to make a greater difference. The next Monday, however, those who had debated so pessimistically were back in their rooms trying again to make the difference.

It is inconceivable that we would have said to ourselves, 'These kids are condemned. There's nothing I can do. I might as well put my feet up and read the paper while they waste their time.' We struggled. Like thousands before and since, if we changed our attitudes at all in response to our dismal calculations, it was to try harder rather than to give up. Those who felt like giving up changed their job. For as long as I have been a teacher, most teachers of deprived children have had a commitment, a commitment not to an ideal, or to a social class, but to the individual young people with whom they work. I want a future for Dionne and Dean, for Dawn and Desmond, and I believe their futures will be largely determined by their educational success. This is how inner city teachers feel about their work and their pupils.

This does not prevent us from being realistic. If Dean is 15, has problems reading *The Mirror* and hates being asked, attends school sporadically, is well known to the Metropolitan Police, and has absolutely no connections which could find him employment nor any inclination to go to college, we are entitled to doubt that he is about to become part of a can-do culture. We are also entitled to ask how he got here, and entitled to believe that the answer does not start and end with incompetent primary teachers, bad schools, and negative attitudes excusing failure.

We also know that Dean has received far more resources than the average for a state educated pupil: not only small group work for his reading, but hours of one-to-one pastoral support, and the services at times of an educational psychologist and the education welfare officer. Perhaps these resources have not been well directed. Perhaps Dean's teachers could have been more effective, if they had used other techniques, although I have showed previously that teachers are scarcely autonomous professionals when it comes to such things.

Government rhetoric is not about that, however: it asserts that achievement in the inner city is significantly depressed by teachers finding excuses for failure. To look for explanations for Dean's failure is not to excuse it, but to seek to prevent the failure being repeated by his children. Teachers come to believe that the overwhelming reasons for failure are located *outside the school*, not in order to displace responsibility, but because that is the lesson of their experience of the pupils they get to know so well. The techniques that have failed with Dean have been successful with other children from more favoured backgrounds in other kinds of schools.

The government, however, professes a single, simple strategy for helping Dean, and all the Deans. Schools must be improved — or, to be more accurate, schools must improve themselves. Educational failure is the fault of schools; there is nothing more to be said. The government repeats this one notion as loudly and as often as possible, and closes debate by declaring that those who are not with us are against us. It then puts into effect a series of policies aimed at school improvement. Let us examine the effectiveness of these policies.

League tables

At the heart of the drive for improvement is the continuation of the central strategy of the previous government, which is the operation of a market mechanism. The central components of the mechanism are local management of schools, which allocates funding very largely on a per pupil basis, parental choice, and wide publication of results. The intended effect is competition between schools. It is taken for granted that this mechanism is working. After all, results are improving year on year. To question it is, indeed, a declaration of negativity and opposition to education. I have to question it.

The degree of improvement in achievement, particularly in terms of formal qualifications at 16+, is always the subject of great debate, with researchers unable to make comparisons over long periods because of the continual changes in the content and methods of examinations. Nevertheless, it is incontrovertible that, nationally, GCSE results improve year by year. However, whereas the school market mechanism has been operating for less than ten years, improvements in 16+ results have been virtually continuous throughout my career of almost thirty years, and indeed longer than that. Indeed, research suggests that in areas of the country where competition is strongest, GCSE results improve by less than average, and that where competition does not operate, results improve by more than average. Scotland and Northern Ireland, for example, have not adopted the English model, but yet are showing improvements at least as impressive as those in England. In short, there is no evidence that the market mechanism works to improve achievement.

However, this does not mean that the mechanism has had no effects on schools. Despite the widespread, though not universal, scepticism in schools, headteachers in general feel they have to play the game, and watch the league tables. Each year, the government eggs on the media to make a meal of the results, and newspapers comply by the acre. Of the whole range of statistics which might be used to portray a school, the one — the only one — highlighted, the one which is now the common currency for describing school achievement, is the percentage of pupils achieving five GCSEs at grades A-C.

I have already described some ways in which schools respond to this, in particular the concentration of resources on pupils at the grade C/D boundary. The messages of rejection to those below that boundary are a particularly negative outcome of the league table system.

The government has decided to overcome this problem by replacing the five A-C count with a point system which gives credit for achievement at all grades in a way similar to the generally accepted points score for A level results. It will solve one problem, but is certain to create unintended others. For example, pupils are likely to be entered for exams for which they are unsuited in the hope they will accumulate at least some points score. This is nothing but a restatement of the obvious, that teachers will always feel obliged to teach to the test. The mode and prominence of assessment will always drive the curriculum.

A widely accepted way to make league tables more realistically reflect school achievement is to establish 'value-added' measurements of pupil attainment. The problem with this idea, to which all of the great and the good within education seem to be committed, is that it is always just about to be introduced, but never quite appears. This is despite a number of years spent by a number of people on devising value-added measures. Some of us doubt whether such measurements are possible in practice, or even in theory.

The most simplistic version, the one introduced by the Qualifications and Curriculum Authority, is the most questionable. In this model, the value added to a pupil's attainment in any given Key Stage is the number of national curriculum (NC) levels gained. But how many subjects are we counting? Perhaps we should restrict ourselves to the core subjects — but where does that leave the pupil who makes modest improvement in those, but whose, say, artistic talents are uncovered and brought to flower by the school?

More importantly, this method would only be statistically valid if we assume that to raise every child by 1 NC level required the same input, the same amount of teacher time, skill, and patience. Any teacher of a year 7 class some of whom are working at level 2 in English knows that her chances of getting them to level 3 are somewhat less than getting others to improve from level 5 to 6. No, the fact is that the NC level descriptions were not designed with such a purpose in mind, and are not fit to be used as a statistical tool. But to education administrators, and perhaps even some researchers, the tempting availability of numbers resulting from NC assessments, and the unfortunate lack of any alternative, moves them towards that very application which they must know is without foundation. When challenged, they may say words to the effect that it's the best measurement we have, and we must move forward on this. It is not necessary to be a committed phenomenologist to protest against such an unsustainable method.

The more difficult theoretical question is whether the value added is measurable at all. Doubters should be charitable about the language. The terminology is unfortunate, but does not necessarily mean that those who use it see children as a commodity, the school as a factory, and the end result as an economic unit. Nevertheless, they are open to the charge that they are simplifying the process and outcomes of schooling to the point of total distortion.

To make that charge is not to propose that measurable outcomes are not important. It is to propose that it is impossible to quantify the input which has produced that outcome. It's like a business in which the unit cost of production varies because of variations in the quality of the raw materials or components which are beyond the control of the producer. That comparison cannot take us far, however, because in that business it may be possible to measure the amount of extra labour and materials which are required to raise a batch of the raw material to the necessary quality. In education, it would be impossible in practice to monitor the work done in the same way.

Perhaps the major difficulty with the value-added concept is that some of the outcomes of schooling which are desired by society, as well as by Ofsted, are just not measurable. The areas we may describe as personal, social and moral education seem to be growing in importance in the minds of public and politicians as moral panic succeeds moral panic about the condition of our society. The responsibility of schools in these matters is indeed a strong component of our tradition of working class education, and probably marks out our system from that in some other countries. But short of administering a test to each school leaver on 'Ten Ways to Give Your Partner a Better Orgasm' (which of course they will have covered the previous week in their teen mag), it is not possible to measure these things.

Probably the only way we can know anything about our success in these areas is to meet our ex-pupils on the street, perhaps with their partners and children, and find that they have developed successful lives. This, incidentally, remains one of the rewards of teaching which almost makes up for everything else, and which no-one has yet worked out a way of taking from us.

None of this should detract from the use of value-added analysis in certain, limited, ways. It is possible to analyse the progress of a large population, say a national cohort, in terms of certain specific and limited aspects of achievement, and to tease out some interesting statistical relationships. Indeed, I quoted an example earlier.

What is important is to recognise the limits of its utility, and to recognise it as incapable of generating useful judgements about the quality of individual schools, despite its superficial attraction as an alternative to the crude performance table approach which currently operates. Unfortunately, neither the crude approach nor a more sophisticated approach actually produces results of any validity. Quite apart from all the other problems, the size of the population, an age cohort in a single school, is too small from a statistical point of view.

If all society wants from schools is a guarantee of basic literacy and numeracy skills, then test them only, and the English will become more literate and numerate and very uneducated. If society wants young people qualified in academic disciplines defined over a century ago, then publish the results of our current exam system. But if society wants young people with a broad education to meet the needs of contemporary society and economy, it must recognise that an obsession with a narrow range of exam statistics has to end.

A critique of the local management of schools is beyond the scope of this book. I comment elsewhere on parental choice. The use of league tables has negative effects. Put together, these three features constitute a market mechanism that is not working, and there is no evidence that competition improves school performance. While it remains, however, it continues to be damaging to inner city schools and their teachers, and prevents coherent policies for supporting underclass schools.

As I described earlier, the real effect of the market mechanism is to increase the social polarisation of school intakes, so that 'good' schools find it easy to 'improve', while 'poor' schools struggle against ever increasing odds. Of course we cannot address this issue as long as we remain in denial of the realities of the relationship between intake and performance, and neither can we make significant inroads into the long tail of underachievement.

The add-ons

There is one policy area which the government can claim is designed to discriminate positively in favour of the further-to-go school. That is the promotion of a range of provision outside the normal school sessions to support learning. I refer here to homework clubs, revision centres, summer schools, and the like.

There is no doubt at all in my mind that such provision makes a difference. As I have described, most of these ideas have been tried, particularly in inner city schools. In London, after-school centres and Easter revision centres are long-standing traditions. The problem with their adoption as a political priority is that the government's zero tolerance of dissent makes it more difficult to make balanced and restrained judgements on their effects.

They provide a safe and caring environment which may be far superior to the alternative, but let us leave out of the equation this social service aspect, which for younger children is often dominant. Let us concentrate on the difference made to educational achievement.

It is unfortunate that when the government sponsored some pilot summer schools, it announced their success before the evaluation was carried out, because again sensible debate on whether they represented value for money was closed down. At least there was an evaluation, which made modest claims for the learning advantages to the youngsters who took part. What was missing was follow-up to attempt to discover whether the effects were long-term.

A problem in secondary age provision is attracting to it those who need it most. My own children were quite happy to use the Easter revision centre at their school just before their GCSEs, but their classmates who lacked motivation and could have been helped to pick up a grade or two here and there could not be persuaded to sign up. In the underclass school, cajoling a group of pupils to stay at school for longer on a regular basis is an exhausting task in itself.

These extras are expensive. The only way they can be organised effectively is by the employment of staff completely separate from the school staff, not least because, as I have shown, the school staff are already overstretched and overworked. The teacher unions are somewhat antagonistic to this development because they suspect the government will try to implement it on the cheap by changing teachers' conditions of service to require them to work the extra hours, and they point to a miserly extra payment already introduced for the work. Teachers would just not put up with such an extension, and the government must realise as much.

The extras are expensive, then, and have a marginal effect, and only on a small proportion of the target pupils. Hence, a realistic assessment would weigh up the cost/benefits of this policy as against the injection of the same sums into the schools themselves. I believe that the assessment would show that homework clubs and the like can make a significant difference to some individual pupils, but are not an efficient answer for the bulk of those inner city pupils who are antagonistic to education. In short, they are no substitute for investment in the schools.

Fresh Start

Fresh Start is not really a new idea. It has operated, in different ways, and for different reasons, for many years. So there is plenty of evidence as to its utility. The conclusion to be drawn is that, on occasion, it might work. Generally it does not. And it leaves a very real question as to whether the upheaval and pain is worth the result.

The concept of Fresh Start is simple. A school which is failing, and where all efforts to improve it have failed, is closed down. A new school is opened on the same site. It is new because it has a new name, and new staff. I am not sure that the idea has been developed any further than that. For those who have followed the argument of this book, the not inconsiderable flaw is obvious.

The main determinant of the failing inner city school is the intake. Where the intake is largely from the underclass, a school has very little chance of not 'failing' within the terms of the current debate. Hence, to give a school a fresh start, it is more important to change the pupil mix than to change the staff or the name. It is not clear that admissions policy is on anyone's agenda at the moment.

However, as pragmatists, teachers would prefer to examine how it has worked in practice than to spend too much time on the theory. It is secondary schools which have been subject to rebirths. In the past, a very similar process occurred when schools were reorganised because of falling rolls. Many cities had to deal with significant reductions in the numbers of children, particularly in the seventies and eighties.

In inner London, for example, although the problem was resolved partly through closures, the main technique was amalgamation. There were some parallels between Fresh Start and these amalgamations, which involved two or sometimes three schools. The school whose premises became the main or sole site of the new school was frequently considered to be the one taking over the other, but great efforts were made to overcome that tendency. Often, the new school would have a new headteacher, with those from the closing schools redeployed or retired. Obviously, the trappings such as name and uniform were new.

The difference between amalgamation and Fresh Start was that the bulk of the staff were not new. Some staff were displaced from their posts, but the new school's staffing levels were reduced by natural wastage or, later, redeployment. Another important feature was the kinds of schools which were combined. For some odd reason, the ILEA seldom proposed to touch the grammar schools, or former grammar schools as they became in the mid seventies, which were at the top of the city's pecking order. To a certain extent, this produced or sustained distortions of the social mix which persist to the present day, and in part allowed the persistence of the sink school.

For example, one of the schools for the underclass which has been an exemplar at a number of places in this book has been amalgamated twice. Yet on neither occasion was it proposed to join with the very prestigious grammar school which was just two hundred yards away. Instead, it was joined with other underclass schools further away. Naturally, this school had changes of headteacher, changes of staff, changes of uniform — and the same intake, producing the same problems.

However, in most cases, amalgamating schools were in different positions within the hierarchy. In other words, the new school's intake was a social mix. In other words, given a fair wind, the school could succeed. Naturally, a very strong determinant was the quality of the headteacher.

Of course, the circumstances of amalgamation are different from those applying to the Fresh Start, but the lessons do illuminate the debate. Is there a reasonable social mix? Is the new headteacher up to it? They were the key questions then. As we shall see, they are the key questions now.

There has been a variety of responses by local authorities to the Ofsted failure of secondary schools. In some instances, it has provided a simple solution to a continuing problem of over-provision, being an unanswerable justification for closure. In other cases, very considerable resources have been allocated to the schools in an attempt to improve those results which are measured by Ofsted. Elsewhere, however, Fresh Start has been operated. Let us look at two case studies.

Battersea Technology College

Battersea Technology College, in Wandsworth, is an extremely instructive example. Battersea County, as it was known for a long time, is a long-standing school for the underclass. Even under an outstanding head, some twenty years ago, the school struggled, and it was certainly a struggle to work there.

When taken over by Wandsworth Council in 1990, Battersea Park, as it was then called after another amalgamation, came to the attention of the innovative Donald Naismith, the borough's interesting Director of Education. The council might be pilloried for avoiding its responsibility for planning and co-ordinating secondary school provision, which it achieved by positively encouraging the bulk of its schools to opt out of local authority control. The result was a frustrating (for parents) and damaging (for the education community) free-for-all at 11+, and the impossibility of doing anything at council level about the mix of the intake to Battersea Park School.

However, the council did anything but leave the school to wither. Closure was not a realistic option. It would have left the north of the borough without a secondary school. So, since 1990, the school has had not one, but two, fresh starts.

The first was at least as comprehensive as anything suggested by Michael Barber or David Blunkett. At around this time, the Conservative government's (ultimately failing) City Technology College initiative was under way. As independent schools, though fully funded by the state except for a small proportion of initial capital costs, the CTCs were trying all sorts of new practices unfettered by local authority arrangements or national pay and conditions for staff.

As Battersea's new name suggests, some of these ideas attracted the attention of Naismith. Renaming it Battersea Technology College was just the start. Recognising the significance of headship, the authority employed head-hunters to find the successful person who could lead the college into a new era. The head-hunters turned up Michael Clark, from a school on Tyneside. Mr. Clark then fronted a complete transformation of the school.

Wandsworth showed its commitment to the project by spending £2 million on new building at the site. A rather grand new reception area involved resiting the entrance to the school. Splendid new offices were added. Setting the tone for many schools' priorities under local management, a glossy new public image was the priority.

Mr. Clark planned, and the authority implemented, a radical new staffing structure. Unusual at the time, though increasingly popular since, it abolished the traditional distinction between academic and pastoral responsibilities. There were to be no heads of department, or heads of year. Instead, there were to be heads of faculties, and heads of subject. These staff were to be responsible for both the academic and pastoral care of their pupils, and for small devolved budgets. Sceptical staff wondered how the work of the faculties was to be co-ordinated or, to put it another way, how the needs of the whole pupil were to be met but it was easy to dismiss these grumbles as defensiveness from those worried (realistically, as it turned out) that they would lose their jobs.

Unlike the previous employer, the ILEA, Wandsworth refused to guarantee the employment of existing staff, and indeed many failed to get a job in the new structure. Bright, enthusiastic newcomers were brought in at all levels to operate the new college. As the unions were told, the failed teachers of the old regime had to go — the pupils of Battersea Technology College deserved the best, and old-fashioned staffing practices which protected staff at the expense of the pupils were no longer tolerable.

But all this was not sufficient.

The change which finally emphasised the newness of Battersea Tech was the decision to move to a five-term year. Naturally, every other state school in the vicinity remained on the standard three terms, with half-term breaks, with standard dates agreed five years in advance by London authorities collectively. Battersea Tech, however, was to move to eight-week terms, without a mid-term break, and roughly two-week holidays between each term.

This is not the place to discuss the merits of the five-term year as a concept. The structure of the school year has been raised from time to time, with arguments for a variety of patterns. The one thing which is universally accepted is that any radical change would need to be implemented simultaneously across the country. Many groups and interests would suffer from a variety of very different terms — not least parents. It was for those kinds of reasons that the five-term year was opposed. The grumbles of the staff were discounted — it was simply luddism.

The five-term year commenced. The quality of the school's leadership was brought into focus when the unions explained to Mr. Clark that his staff were employed to teach 190 days in a year, that they would teach 190 days, but that Mr. Clark had organised the pupils to attend for 200 days. What frightened some was that Mr. Clark was surprised. Staff had been wondering how the school would organise in the light of these facts. What shook them was that the headteacher clearly had been unaware of them.

After a pause, the masterly solution was produced. The timetable would be suspended for a month during the year. For the first two weeks, half the staff would be on leave, while the other half organised various activities for the pupils. For the second two weeks, the other half of the staff would be on leave. At that moment, everyone knew: the overwhelming requirement of a fresh start, a head who could cut the mustard, was missing.

But the new broom had swept clean. All the bright ideas now called Fresh Start had been put into place. Battersea County had metamorphosed into Battersea Technology College.

The result: disaster.

Just before Christmas 1993, the new showpiece was inspected by Ofsted. It was found to be in need of special measures. Apart from describing the low levels of achievement, the inspectors reported: 'In many lessons and around the school, students' behaviour is too often poor. There is widespread verbal abuse and physical contact (pushing and hitting) among students. Students are reluctant to settle down in lessons, with much excessive noisy disruption and rudeness towards teachers.' After pointing out a number of subject areas where behaviour was better, the inspectors noted that there was a clear system of rewards and punishments, and that 'Standards of behaviour in the college are adversely affected by a number of factors outside the direct control of staff...' My interpretation of this analysis is: poor pupil behaviour is brought into the college from outside, and, despite appropriate policies, only superteachers are able to exercise control.

In truth, the school was in no worse condition than it had been prior to its relaunch. The problems of attendance, order, lack of commitment, amongst the pupils were just the same. The kinds of scene described in Chapter 1 remained commonplace. Often, large numbers of pupils were in the school's public places during lessons. The major difference now was that the staff had to contend with the miseries of special measures.

Wandsworth is not the kind of council to dither. It felt it had to take decisive action. It soon accepted the explanation of HMI and its own inspectorate: the school was failing because the staff, including the leadership, was not up to the necessary standard.

Of course, it was not its style for the Council to admit it had made a monumental error in selecting the headteacher, especially since, not long before, Mr. Clark had featured in a television documentary on how a whizzo can turn round a school. Mr. Clark left quietly. The terms on which he left, and indeed the terms on which he arrived, were never revealed, but many of those involved with BTC guessed that the departure of the general who, above all others, was responsible for the debacle was rather more comfortable than the treatment given to some of the infantry whose working lives were hell.

Now, under a new Director of Education, Wandsworth decided that what BTC needed was... yes, a fresh start. Only this time, a real fresh start. It explained that the problem had been the failure to root out teachers who were not up to the particular challenges the school offered. As the unions were told, the failed teachers of the old regime had to go — the pupils of Battersea Technology College deserved the best, and old-fashioned staffing practices which protected staff at the expense of the pupils were no longer tolerable.

This time, the council was determined to do a thorough job. Bob Pope arrived from a school in Croydon. His remit, it transpired, was temporary: to supervise the new fresh start, whilst a new superhead was recruited.

The acting head, with the same inspectors who had approved the previous structure, worked out yet another staffing structure. The manifest problems of the previous one were addressed, and a much more typical structure resulted. This was approved by the same governors who had approved the disastrous predecessor just a few months previously. This time, every single post in the school was deemed to be deleted, and every single teacher was required to apply for a new post, even if some of them were suspiciously similar. Any teacher unsuccessful at interview would be redundant.

This was to be a fresh start with a vengeance. This kind of restructuring is, of course, a part of the flexible working practices so beloved of the government, and common throughout business. It has also become increasingly common in schools and, particularly, colleges.

It is true to say, however, that in education the process continues to meet real resistance from staff, and the unions which represent them. The restructuring proposal at BTC was resisted. It was argued that the staff were being made to pay for the mistakes of the council, the governors and the management. It was argued that if there were any staff who were really not competent, there were procedures for dealing with them, and the unions would co-operate. It was argued that the restructuring process would both preoccupy and demoralise the staff, so that the pupils would suffer further. All this was argued, without any success whatsoever. In the spring of 1995, the restructuring took place.

It is difficult to know how much of a clear out the council intended. The result was that 26 of the 30 teaching staff left that summer. Many of them were indeed too demoralised to stay. They found jobs in more amenable surroundings, or they took the severance and early retirement packages on offer, some more reluctantly than others. Only two were finally subjected to compulsory redundancy.

Many of the posts, particularly at classroom teacher level, had to be filled by external advertisement and the recruitment of newly qualified teachers. In September 1995, in other words, there was an almost completely new staff, many inexperienced in teaching, or inexperienced in the particular problems of a school for the underclass.

As explained earlier, schools for the underclass are kept afloat only by a group of experienced staff who know the school and its pupils. It needs senior staff who can walk into a classroom and see at once which pupils do not belong there. No school can succeed without some stability amongst its staff, and this requirement is strongest where it is met least: in the school for the underclass.

The staff at BTC were new. However, it had the same pupils.

For those who argue for Fresh Start and similar tactics on the grounds that each child has only one chance, and we must act immediately, some of the results of this are interesting. Those who complained most were the parents of pupils moving into year 11. Many of them had a completely new set of teachers half way through their GCSE course. However good the records left behind, it is always difficult for a teacher to pick up a GCSE group with, effectively, two terms of the course left. If there is no-one else in the department who knows the pupils and the systems, the task is doubly difficult. If there are no systems, because the whole department is new, the struggle is uphill. If all this is occurring in a school for the underclass, where pupil commitment is minimal, the hill becomes a cliff. And finally, if this is happening in every subject on a pupil's timetable, any realistic observer could expect 'nul points' in the following year's GCSE league table.

The results of this fresh fresh start were predictable, if not predicted. The following summer, just 5% of pupils achieved higher GCSE grades. This may have been an improvement on the previous two years of upheaval, but scarcely justified the upheaval.

Yet even this was not the end of the instability. The new new headteacher, Andrew Poole, took up post in September 1996. It was only then that HMI, in their regular monitoring visit, sensed that the school was starting to develop a sense of direction and development. At the end of his first year, there was little outward sign of improvement: 5% of pupils achieved the magic 5 A-C grades at GCSE, the same as in the previous year.

Apparently worse, there was yet another exodus of staff, with some 60% of the new new staff leaving. Yet Mr. Poole had some justification for telling the local press that many improvements were in place, and that the school was on the way up. The school was becoming noticeably more orderly, allowing improvements to teaching and learning. Strategies for interventions with pupils were in hand. Attendance improved from a disastrous 70% to 85%. Mr. Poole, in a quiet way, went out selling the school in the local estates, and in the next two years the number of applications at 11+ increased dramatically.

After more than four years, Battersea Tech remains on special measures, although the fact it was not 'named and shamed' in the summer of 1997, despite fulfilling all the criteria, suggests that HMI considered it to be on the road to recovery, and it is expected to be taken off special measures during 1998. Yet the school is a completely different institution from the one which Wandsworth inherited in 1990. It has new buildings, new leadership, a completely new staff (almost none of the teachers now in the school was there in 1993), new name, new uniform. How can it be that repeatedly getting rid of all the people who, we are told, were not good enough, and all their baggage, achieved nothing for so long? All that effort, all that heartache, all those professional lives and pupil careers disrupted, for what gain?

The only variable that has remained constant is the pupil intake. Is there really no lesson here? Further light on this question may be cast by an examination of a second case, that of the Phoenix School, in the borough of Hammersmith and Fulham.

Phoenix School

Phoenix is probably the school that would spring to mind first as a successful example of Fresh Start. It, or rather its headteacher, has featured in all the posh papers. The story has been told, again and again, as a simple 'before and after'.

The 'before' is a state of disorder, an Ofsted inspection, special measures. The turning point is the appointment of William Atkinson as headteacher. The 'after' is onwards and upwards to a new Labour promised land of successful schools for all, intake no excuse, an orderly learning environment.

Now, my sophisticated reader, you may well ask whether the papers have got it right. What is the *real* Phoenix story?

Hammersmith School was always a typical example of the schools which are the focus of this book. Very largely serving the huge council housing estate in which it is situated, through ups and downs, amalgamations and changes, it was always a difficult school. Like Battersea County, in the good times it kept its head above water, and in the bad times it did not.

The early nineties were one of the bad times. The outstanding issue was a senior management which could not manage the situation. Some reports have suggested that the problem, then and later, was exacerbated by the obstructive attitude of the staff, as represented by their unions.

The opposite is true. As in all failing schools with inadequate management, the staff were crying out for leadership and order. Of course they were frustrated that they did not feel supported when dealing with unacceptable behaviour. Of course the frustrations were expressed negatively at times, and as behaviour spiralled downwards the frustrations grew.

Stress and exhaustion produced high levels of absence; supply teachers came, could not cope, and did not stay; the newly qualified staff who filled the gaps only rarely survived; the old stagers retreated to their classrooms, and held the line in their own small castles.

In the absence of action from above, some of the experienced staff tried to implement their own improvement strategies. For example, in an attack on the 'detention — we just don't turn up' problem, a rota of staff collected pupils from the classrooms at the end of the day.

The Ofsted inspection in February 1994, with its inevitable label of 'failing', alerted the local authority to the need for action. Hammersmith and Fulham's Director of Education, the forceful Christine Whatford, herself a former secondary head, has developed a reputation for impatience with poor performance by headteachers. Reacting immediately to the inspection report's adverse comment on the senior management, the authority removed the school's delegated powers and removed the head.

The key change, and the media have it right here, was the appointment of the new headteacher. Having taken the wise precaution to ascertain that he would be supported by the authority in that most important way, with the chequebook, Mr. Atkinson took up post after Easter 1994.

It was he who instituted some other changes which give the appearance of Fresh Start. He needed the authority to fund a clean-up of the buildings and site before his arrival, and a later series of minor building works, to brighten the school and improve the orderly circulation of pupils. The highly symbolic new name and new uniform which followed were strong messages to the estate and the borough that things were changing, and that parents should choose this new school.

If this kind of repackaging, and much greater expenditure, were unsuccessful in recreating Battersea Tech, how was Phoenix different? The answer lies very largely with the headteacher. Mr. Atkinson is a highly skilled and very vigorous self-publicist, and attended directly to the need in the current environment for schools to attract pupils in sufficient numbers and quality.

He made sure that he became visible on the streets round the school. Planning his excursions for maximum impact, and using his walkie-talkie as a dramatic prop, the mythology soon grew that he was everywhere. From arresting pupils found in the wrong place, to visiting parents to persuade them to work with the school, he created an image of dynamism, change, demands on pupils and expectations of parents. The local press was used in the same way. Phoenix School has indeed been reinvented in the minds of the local community, as the steady increase in roll indicates. However, and crucially, the image of the school is bound up entirely with its leader. As always, charismatic leadership carries with it the inevitable problem of succession.

The image of dynamic ubiquity was created even more strongly within the school. The media report accurately the long hours worked by the head-teacher — just as long, in fact, as the average head, according to government figures, and just as long as his subordinates in the school.

Mr. Atkinson established systems for every school activity. They amount to a hierarchy of relentless pressure. The head, it is believed, sees everything, and holds a member of staff responsible for it. A piece of litter on a classroom floor? Down the line of management goes the demand to be told who is the culprit — not the pupil who dropped it, but the teacher who did not notice it, or did not deal with it. A pupil will be stopped in the corridor. No homework written in the proper place in the pupil's diary? What teacher is responsible for the omission?

But what about the staff? As we have seen, the Wandsworth approach was to link Fresh Start to the apparent need for a fresh staff. The responsibility for failure was laid with the classroom teachers whose results were so poor. But Hammersmith and Fulham did not take that view. Christine Whatford believed that the authority's role was to put in place quality leadership, and to support the headteacher's management of quality issues within the staff. There was no clearout, no redundancy, no message of collective incompetence — and, to that extent, no Fresh Start.

It is true that the Atkinson processes of relentless pressure were focused particularly, in the early days, on one or two teachers who seemed to him not capable of coming to terms with his requirements. They left. 'Did they fall, or were they pushed?' comes to mind.

Large numbers of other teachers have left in the period since the arrival of the head, including some who have come and gone during that time. However, the pattern is not radically different from the turnover typical of difficult inner London schools, and is hardly surprising within the context of the relentless pressure policy. Deputy heads and faculty heads are particularly prone to turn in exhaustion to the back pages of the Times Educational Supplement, frustrated by the lack of autonomy within their own areas of responsibility.

The staff are noticeably ambiguous about their leadership. Mr. Atkinson has been responsible for restoring an environment of order. That is not to say that control is not a problem in classrooms. It is to say that classroom teachers have the backup of effective systems for dealing with disorderly pupils. The headteacher is not squeamish about excluding permanently those who do not meet his standards, and the question of whether a school is a net donor or net recipient of excluded pupils is a vital determinant of failure.

For those who worked at the school previously, this is the all-important advance. Mr. Atkinson is also responsible for improvements to the buildings, and for improving the number and balance of the intake, which if sustained can push the school up the hierarchy.

And yet, and yet... staff cannot help resenting the relentless pressure strategy. At one level, teachers with responsibilities do not have the authority to exercise their judgements, as even minor decisions have to be referred through a chain of command to the head. More significantly, all teachers are pressured to work to a level which is unreasonable to expect, and, for many, physically just cannot be sustained. Hence the turnover.

Of course, improving exam results justify relentless pressure. In 1994, only

11% of pupils gained 5 A-Cs at GCSE. By 1997, this figure had risen to... 16%. Even then, the headteacher was warning of a likely downturn in results. After all, of the intake of 1994, who will become GCSE statistics in 1999, some 40% were tested as being within the bottom 2% of attainment nationally.

So a charismatic and apparently successful headteacher, with a staff willing, for a certain period of time, to be driven, pushed and harassed, have improved exam results from rock bottom to a level which is typical of a school judged by HMI to be in need of special measures. All that sweat, oh yes and tears... for that? And the question that everyone asks at Phoenix remains: what will become of the school after Atkinson?

Learning from Fresh Start

What conclusions are to be drawn from these case studies regarding the utility of the concept of Fresh Start? The first is that the failure of inner city schools cannot be explained in terms of incompetent staff. As described previously, teachers in these schools may not be executing lessons of the kind and quality expected by some inspector from another planet, but that is not because of their lack of professionalism but because of the real situation they find themselves in.

Quite apart from any empirical observation, the idea seems unlikely. What subscribers to this view have never been able to explain is the process by which, in some strange accident or malevolent design, incompetent teachers are all attracted to particular schools. Everyone knows that some of the people in the profession ought not to be there, because they simply do not have the personal qualities necessary. The question for analysts of failing schools is, how does it come to pass that such teachers end up disproportionately in such schools? Experienced teachers have always known that this is simply not the case. Now the evidence of Fresh Starts confirms it. Despite repeated attempts to change the staff, those brought in to schools for the underclass are no more able to transform pupil outcomes than those they replace. The first lesson is that it is not the teachers, it is the situation which creates failure.

The second conclusion is about leadership. As previously discussed, the leadership of the headteacher is at least as crucial in a school for the underclass as in any other school. The difference is, the job is beyond most people who try it.

We may presume that those headhunted have been successful, in terms of conventional measurements, in previous schools. At least, let me put it another way: those schools have been successful with those heads in place, and they have plausibly claimed some credit. And yet, in one of the cases studied, no fewer than three heads were unable to make the necessary difference, and the jury is out on the fourth. There are many other examples to hand of successful professionals whose careers were buried in sand when they took up headship posts in schools for the underclass.

The other case shows clearly that such a post can only be filled satisfactorily by a superhead, one with charisma who can dominate pupils. The worry is the classical one surrounding the exercise of charismatic authority: what happens when the leader departs? I, for one, have deep fears for the future of Phoenix when Mr. Atkinson moves on.

In short, there is a massive problem about finding suitable leaders for schools for the underclass. Very, very few have the capacity to succeed. A school which is lucky enough to find one might look up and, in the present scenario, even escape special measures. History teaches us that the school will sink back into the mire when that head leaves.

The problem is compounded by the lack of any method yet found to select superheads, and the difficulty of persuading those who might fit the bill to apply for headship. The third component of the problem is the continuing concentration on inappropriate criteria for selecting heads for such schools.

There is no evidence that the superficial trappings, such as changing the name or uniform, have any beneficial effect, despite the rumour that some parents in Southwark chose the failing school William Penn because it had been renamed Dulwich High and they confused it with Dulwich College. On the contrary, the evidence of many years, for example from amalgamations, is that changing the name, in itself, has no effect on parental perception.

Fresh Start is a political gimmick. It is of a piece with recent education policy; presented with gloss and glitz, but ignoring all the hard questions which teachers and administrators have been struggling with for years. It's like undoing the gorgeous wrapping of a Christmas present and finding nothing inside. Fresh Start gives the impression of decision and action. It causes considerable disruption. It achieves nothing. We need to look elsewhere for answers to a perennial problem.

Education Action Zones

The Education Action Zone (EAZ) is another controversial attempt to intervene in schools for the underclass. In principle, the concept could be congruent with the theme of this book, that some schools in the inner city have needs which are qualitatively different from those of the normal school, and special measures of a non-Ofsted kind are needed to deal with them. The question is, exactly what Action is going to take place in these Zones?

I am sure we can understand the government's feeling that it needs to act fast, but the birth of the Zones gives rise to some questions. The Bill providing for their establishment gave little inkling as to the detail of their operation, and detailed regulations were not published at the time when bids were invited. This seems close to a defining example of a pig in a poke, not least because of the conflicting messages from the government at the time about how EAZs might work. What, exactly, is the idea?

One version is the model operating in a number of places in the United States. Some school boards have contracted out their schools lock, stock and barrel to businesses which have promised better results for lower costs. The outcomes have been mixed, but it is not an unfair summary that the output has depended on the input.

As I argue later, there are many measures which could be taken to improve these schools, but many of them depend on radically increased resources, particularly staffing. However, there is one fact of life which seems inescapable: private firms can only continue in existence as long as they make a profit. Profit is an added cost which must make the whole operation more expensive, unless it is offset by reduced costs elsewhere. Reduced costs, in the context of a school where staffing costs comprise 80% — 90% of budget, can only mean reduced staffing — or forcing down staff wages.

In the end, the American experience of privatisation has ended in disappointment, as school boards learn anew that they get nothing for nothing. Some ministers have spoken more warmly than others of private intervention in EAZs, but such full blown privatisation seems unlikely.

Another version seems to be an extension of the principle of sponsorship already at work in the technology schools initiative. Organisations which put up £100,000 helped schools gain 'Technology College Status', and were given seats on the governing body. One controversial example was the involvement of British American Tobacco with a struggling Church of England school in Camberwell. On this model, the sponsors of EAZs are expected to be organisations whose expertise will provide innovatory thinking about the problems faced by the schools in the zone.

The problem with this is that there are no organisations except local education authorities with experience of running this kind of school. Whatever the merits of fresh thinking from outside the system, the fresh thoughts have to be tested against the understanding and experience of those who have coped inside the system over the years. Even after bids had been submitted, there remained considerable doubt about the way the Zones were to be governed and managed, but sponsors as advisers look very different from sponsors as decisive governors.

One consistent theme, however, whichever version is being touted, is the replacement of the local authority by an unelected body, the forum, as the key layer of control. The legislation is extremely vague about the constitution and powers of the forum, and the pilot scheme proposals provide no clarification. After the grant-maintained experience, few teachers would support such a move. Indeed, the evidence of both the Audit Commission and Ofsted is that local authorities in general are doing a good job, and it would seem perverse to remove the essential elements of local knowledge and experience, and local democratic control, from the Zones.

Whitehall's underlying opposition, or at least ambivalence, to local government has long existed, but it has never generated a coherent argument for reform. An EAZ forum can only be an expensive and inefficient duplication of administration and management. Local authorities are not crying wolf when they protest that they cannot support their schools for the underclass in ways they would like because of want of resources, and the restrictions of formula funding on allocating what they have. Within local authorities there are managers who are quite capable of imaginative innovation in their schools, if only they are given resources and the legal framework.

If the initiative is interpreted as an attempt to inject additional funds into these schools, the idea would be very largely supported. However, the injection is subject to a bidding system. Bidding in this way is becoming increasingly discredited as a mechanism for allocating public sector funds, partly because bid-writing becomes an excessively time-consuming exercise, particularly for the unsuccessful, and because allocations are made on the basis of the best bid-writer rather than the greatest need. In this case, some schools will have access to extra money, while other schools not far away with equal or greater need will get none. This inequality gives rise to resentments.

Worse, when the razzmatazz is stripped away, the amounts of money reaching each school are extremely marginal. The million pounds allocated to each Zone has other uses.

The appointment of a highly paid Zone manager, and other costs of running the Zone, will take a large proportion of the money available. One quarter of the funding is from business. In almost every case, this funding will be entirely in kind, in the forms of IT and other equipment or 'management time'. The exception is the contract in Barnsley whereby the education business Nord Anglia will receive £400,000 for consultancy and monitoring services.

In most cases, much of the remainder is to be used for 'add-ons' — the activities before and after school, and in the holidays, which are allegedly innovative but are already commonplace. In many Zones, there will also be some additional staff for specialist projects. Another feature is schemes for family literacy.

This spending on the peripherals is typical of the reluctance of decision makers to confront the site of the action — the classroom. As I have shown, the classroom of the underclass school is no place for learning, and all the money spent on homework clubs, summer schools and the like will make no impact on that central issue.

It is true that many of the Zones will experiment with curriculum for older pupils, and this is likely to make some difference. As I explain later, however, this merely allows a few schools to revert to the more dynamic condition of curriculum development which existed before the national curriculum strait-jacket.

What schools in the Zones need is more teachers, more books and supplies, better accommodation, more support staff. They need to be able to convert classrooms into places of order and attention. There is nothing in this scheme which impinges on that need. In truth, the EAZ initiative will not inject significant additional funds into schools, but will invent an extra layer of school management — exactly what is not needed.

This squalid attention to cash may seem small-minded; after all, the government is looking for centres of ideas and innovation, with regulatory restrictions on curriculum and teachers removed. I can see this as an exciting possibility, and I invite the EAZs to consider my prescriptions in the following chapters.

Unfortunately, in the current circumstances, almost any innovation will have considerable resourcing implications. Take as an example a new curriculum offer, which may appear to require not so much expenditure as ideas. There are plenty of ideas around, but nobody at present working in an EAZ school has the time to work them up to implementation. Additional teaching staff would have to be employed to make such time available. There is also the expense of teaching materials to be developed or bought.

It must be remembered that under local management of schools formula funding, these schools are generally in perennial financial difficulty. They tend to suffer falling roll which requires annual cuts in spending, and they tend to suffer from the inability of a formula, which in law is supposed to be simple and transparent, to reflect sufficiently sensitively their additional resource needs.

This is why, in itself, the provision for EAZs not to be bound by statutory pay provision seems an irrelevance. The pay scale has eighteen points, but even in London where many schools are desperate for staff virtually no secondary teacher is paid on the top four points (the top six points in primary schools), simply because the schools cannot afford it. In other words, the statutory pay system has flexibility which inner city schools cannot use. One possible innovation which will be beyond EAZ schools would be to offer significantly enhanced pay to recruit the kind of teachers who can survive there.

When the EAZs were announced, the unions reacted negatively, both to the suggestions of privatisation, and to the provision for the suspension of national terms and conditions. On the latter, the main fear was not on the pay front, but that EAZs would increase the number of working days. Of course teachers would want to resist such a worsening, but it is unfortunate that this spectre prevents positive discussion on a range of other innovations which might help teachers and pupils. As mentioned above, the five-term year is an idea worthy of serious consideration. It would have tremendous educational and social ramifications, and needs to be considered coolly. How is that possible when teachers believe it is a back door to the imposition of worse conditions?

The idea that schools serving the underclass should be given an impetus to innovate should be welcomed by all. The overlaying of that idea with some unwelcome baggage, particularly the intervention of private enterprise and the perceived attack on teachers' conditions, makes it difficult for those central to these schools to be positive.

I believe that the EAZs in operation will illustrate again what the Americans are learning: you get nothing for nothing. If the government thinks that these schools can be 'turned round' just by the application of bright ideas brought in by energetic entrepreneurs, it will learn a hard lesson. As I shall now suggest, there are many things that could be done, but they cost.

7

HOW TO IMPROVE THE SCHOOL IN THE CITY

A PURPOSE OF THIS BOOK is to enter the debate about meeting the government's targets for a radical improvement in academic performance by Britain's youngsters. I have attempted to show that if we are to get to a better future, we must be honest about where we are starting from.

Let us now consider how we may improve the school for the underclass.

The first point is that quick fix solutions proposed by politicians are unlikely to be successful. We have the new rhetoric, of zero tolerance of failure and so on, but the fact is that these schools with these young people from these communities have posed the same questions for many years. Through all those years when politicians showed little interest, teachers and many others have been working on answers. The current situation shows that the answers were not good enough, but I think we can assume that most of the simple things have been tried.

The second point is that there is unlikely to be 'the answer'. The problem is complex, the solutions will be many and partial. There are contributions which can be made at all sorts of places. To discuss all of them is beyond the scope of any one book.

My list of methods for improving the school for the underclass may disappoint many. There is nothing new, no bright ideas, no stroke of inspiration. Unfortunately, the glitz and gloss of the propagandists is... just glitz and gloss.

Oppositional young people can only be turned into learners by the presence of a large number of committed staff, teaching appropriate things in an appropriate manner. This is as true now as it has always been, and gimmicks can make little impact on that need. These basics are expensive, but necessary, as long as this kind of pupil is to be found concentrated into a few schools. Let us look at how these basics can be applied in those schools in such ways that they can make some difference to what goes on in classrooms, as well as the corridors and the staff room.

The curriculum

There is the classroom itself. My concentration on descriptions of class-rooms suggests that this is the key location. There are a number of components of what goes on in classrooms which relate to underclass achievement, which need to be addressed. Let us look at both curriculum and (later) pedagogy.

I remain convinced that the introduction of the national curriculum has had an almost wholly negative influence on working class achievement. One of the drawbacks of any national curriculum is that it is necessarily a state curriculum, and an object of immediate concern to politicians.

Historians are already becoming aware that the form of the national curriculum has been determined as much by political forces as by educational debate, and although the two may cross, they seldom run on the same track. We have learnt that its original form owed much to the hairdresser of the Prime Minister of the day. Of course, it is difficult to deny that the state has rights over institutions on which it spends so much, but determination of what is to be taught by means of political point-scoring cannot be the best way to proceed.

However, we have the national curriculum. It has some well-known weak-nesses. Chief amongst them, particularly in the primary phase, was its overcrowding. The grass roots revolt against the early version did lead to a reduction in coverage, but Sir Ron Dearing's suggestion that it would now occupy only 85% of the time in the primary school was treated with some scepticism. Well-founded, as it turns out, because primary classes could only get through the required syllabuses by pressing on at breakneck speed without time for those potentially rewarding by-ways.

We now have research which supports the frequent contention of secondary heads that the average literacy of eleven-year-olds worsened in the nineties: while no causal connection is proven, the chief suspect must be this requirement to press on, press on, which could only mean less time available to work on literacy skills. The reaction has been to impose further change, in the form of relaxation of the national curriculum together with the most specific and detailed demands ever made on English schools for the teaching of literacy and numeracy.

The introduction of a highly prescribed curriculum in primaries did address an important issue. It replaced a wide variety of practice, but in many schools, particularly where pupils still had to be prepared for some kind of 11+ exam, there was a tendency to a limited curriculum. The question is, were there other ways to deal with that issue? The answer belongs to the 'what if' category of debate which might be highly entertaining but is ultimately inconclusive.

I believe that one effect of the imposition of a curriculum has been to remove the issue from the agenda amongst classroom teachers. We teach what we're told to, there's no point in thinking about what we ought to teach. This, in turn, produces curriculum stagnation. As I point out elsewhere, the English education system has been characterised by bottom-up innovation in pedagogy and curriculum.

Enterprising teachers devised syllabuses to suit the needs of their own pupils, and Mode 3 CSE was perhaps the largest crop of this growth. Perhaps some of the ideas were daft, but certainly many of them were very fruitful, and developed our thinking on what the nation's children needed to know and to be able to do. The removal of this right is an element in the deskilling of teachers; more importantly, it cuts out bottom up creative thinking.

The question is, in the future how is curriculum development to take place? Do we rely on the personal whim of some minister of the crown, or some influential adviser? Where are the development projects which used to be turned out by local authority teachers and advisers? The recent stress on centrally determined and enforced curriculum, and now pedagogy, has been influenced by semi-informed comparison with apparently successful competitor economies.

Only now are we starting to ask whether the twenty-first century demands people with the kind of flexibility and creativity which had always been valued by our decentralised, messy, but dynamic curriculum. State equals stasis, perhaps. At last the feeling is growing that the straitjacket of the current version needs to be removed.

It has to be replaced by a statement of a minimum entitlement. It should state what skills, abilities and knowledge it is essential to acquire while in compulsory education. In being minimalist, it must avoid expansion as successive enthusiasts convince us that some other knowledge is desirable. It could include only the basic communication and numeracy skills, or perhaps add some social and ethical understanding that other social institutions seem to have abandoned to schools. It would relinquish the task of describing everything that pupils should learn, and it would leave the bulk of the curriculum for local decision.

Such a move would have two effects of particular importance to the theme of this book. The first is that it would allow the reinstatement of a curriculum which was of use to the young of the underclass in schools which serve them, as indeed it would allow all schools to offer a relevant curriculum.

I use the word 'relevant' deliberately, knowing that it has been used, abused and discredited. In the past, it has been used by those who meant that learning must be based in pupils' own experience. While there is clearly some sense in that, the problem has often been an accompanying glib social theory which leads to a misunderstanding of what pupils' experience is. The greater problem has been that not only was learning based in pupils' own experience, but it never moved on. Clearly, what every subject in the curriculum must do is to extend the young beyond their prior experience, to take them outwards and upwards.

But the abolition of a prescriptive national curriculum would allow a school flexibility about the routes outwards and upwards. Many secondary schools for the underclass could profit from deploying a large number of teachers whose skill and experience was in the teaching of reading and writing, because at the moment a majority of their intake are functionally illiterate, and so are a large proportion of their leavers. Surely, the most important gain for such pupils would be a full literacy.

What other kinds of learning which are particularly valuable for the young of the underclass have been squeezed out by the national curriculum? So often, in the schools I have described, I have been moved to tears by the performance of the pupils in the expressive or performing arts. They need lots of both. These lessons give pupils the chance to work through their feelings, their anger, their frustration, their depression, even their nihilism. They give the pupils opportunities to succeed. In drama, music, or dance, they can succeed in a social project, and learn that not all social interaction has to be negative.

They need craft lessons — not the artificial design-oriented nonsense that currently passes for technology, but the opportunity to use tools and materials other than paper and card to make really useful objects in which they can take pride. Used only to destruction, these pupils need to learn the connections between effort, construction and self-esteem.

They need lots of social and political education — but as a social studies teacher, I would say that. I would only add that no-one should think I mean by political education an explanation of how the House of Commons works. In all their learning, they need not the national curriculum update of what was considered necessary for the boys of the Victorian upper classes, but what has been called really useful knowledge.

Do you, reader, want to argue with me about my (not exhaustive) list of key subjects for the underclass school? Good! That is the point! Debate about curriculum has died, and the health of our schools requires its resurrection, and a more locally determined curriculum. My version of a locally determined curriculum for the underclass school starts from a realistic assessment of pupils' starting points. Of course, it is vital in such schools to retain the flexibility to meet the needs of those who may be at a more advanced level.

The second effect of replacing the national curriculum with a statement of minimum entitlement would be on teachers. Younger teachers have been trained the national curriculum way. Perhaps they do not question the right of the state to dictate what they teach, but I feel that amongst younger teachers there is some resistance to the idea. For only a few is this what might be called principled. For most, it is just a feeling, which grows with experience of the job, that the national curriculum has not quite got it right, and that if it changes it probably still will not be right.

Those of us trained long ago, however, have never recovered from the dismay of being deskilled by being told what to teach instead of deciding for ourselves. Of course, curriculum decisions in English schools have never been on the whim of the individual teacher. There has always been an apparatus of influence, of debate, of collective decision, of some conformity. The loss of this autonomy is a more important factor in the demoralisation of teachers than has been recognised in most quarters.

Local planning of the curriculum can be seen as an inefficient use of teacher time. It must be useful to have national models, which can be taken off the shelf by those inclined. There is, however, all the difference in the world between a model and a prescription. At the moment, curriculum development is a massive bureaucratic and political exercise, very largely top-down. It needs to become again a continual process of interaction between a national model and the best local innovation.

From the point of view of government, this kind of loosening of curriculum control would represent an unwelcome reversal of the continuing trend of the centralisation of powers, largely to unaccountable agencies. More importantly, perhaps, it would create problems with the current national assessment regime. As I argued earlier, there is absolutely no educational justification for the standard assessment, league table approach. On the other hand, a national test of the core skills which I suggest could remain mandatory might meet the requirements of politicians.

Pedagogy

An appropriate curriculum, then, would help. But young people who are already angry about life, and cynical about their life chances, are unlikely to be converted to schooling just because the work is 'relevant'. A simple reason for this is that it is impossible to convince them of anything unless they can be persuaded to listen to the message in the first place. The completion of a task set in a lesson is no evidence that any listening, in a deep sense, has taken place. Pupils can often conform, and do the work set, to a degree which ensures they stay out of trouble, but with complete lack of commitment, without care, and without any learning. Asked about the work in the next lesson, they will barely recall what it was they did, much less recall its point.

So it is pedagogy, in its widest sense, which is at least as important as content. I hate to jump on an apparently reactionary bandwagon, but it does seem to me that the teacher trainers have been missing the point in respect of inner city education. I have a particular problem with many inspectors and advisors working in the inner city, responsible not only the pattern and tone of in-service training, but also for establishing an orthodoxy through the inspection regimes, local and national.

The dominant theories of classroom organisation are predicated on a concept of young people as willing collaborators in learning. Teachers are told, over and over again, that if the lesson has the appropriate content, with the appropriate differentiation and the appropriate methods, it will be attractive to the class. Pupils are seen as basically co-operative, requiring only to be organised and supervised, with a slight input of motivation. Then they will become, oh bliss!, 'active learners', exploring the subject and discovering the world for themselves. On this model, the teacher is a facilitator. This is an assumption behind the multi-activity classroom, so beloved of primary theorists.

It may well be like that in Hazel Grove or Harrogate. It is not like that in Hackney.

One problem with the concept is the implication that a lesson must be as entertaining as the television programmes the pupils will watch for long hours later in the day. Television, of course, is moving to ever greater extremes to attempt to hold the attention of a bored audience, not only in terms of content but in terms of production. Ever shorter scenes, quick cuts, bizarre camera angles, more arresting sound, and a whole array of techniques lead to a product whose gloss and glitz simply cannot be rivalled by a harassed teacher with broken down videos. My inspector colleagues will deny that their concentration on a good lesson as the answer to class management carries the implication I suggest, but I have seen young teachers spend inordinate hours preparing for a single lesson to try to improve its appeal, despite their previous attempts to do this having been unsuccessful in motivating their pupils.

The more telling objection to this method, however, is the error of the basic assumption as far as inner city schools are concerned. It is reasonable to assume that when young people turn on the television, they are at least willing to be diverted by the programme if it can catch their interest. It is not reasonable to assume that when young people from the underclass attend a lesson, the same willingness is there. There are all sorts of reasons why they do attend the lesson, but the wish to join in a great collective learning enterprise is not one of them.

For those without commitment to state education, there is no commitment to learning in the classroom. There is no sharing of the teacher's values about the utility or beauty of that knowledge and skill which has been the content of English education. At the classroom door, there is no embrace, or even acceptance, of the idea that the next hour is to be spent acquiring some of that knowledge and skill. I conclude that what might be called a democratic pedagogy is hopelessly inappropriate for the schools of the underclass.

Actually, I concluded this, in terms of my own classroom practice, many years ago. I did my teaching practice during training in the Home Counties. There, a little firmness secured order and effort. It was poor preparation for my first job, in a huge monocultural school on the outskirts of Liverpool. In my five years there, I tried a succession of teacher styles in an attempt to produce order out of chaos.

The one I call the three Cs was probably the most commonly used in that school and in other schools I have seen and worked in. A combination of cajolery, compromise, and conciliation was used to jolly things along and obtain a reasonable response from most pupils most of the time. The watchword of this method is, 'Avoid confrontation'. I learnt fast, and avoided being assaulted.

Then I caught an infection. It might have been a course, or something I read. I performed the great liberal experiment.

'Now listen class, you're here for your benefit, not mine. It's up to you to take responsibility for your own learning. It's up to you to decide the rules in this class. I'll provide the facilities, I'll guide you, but you must make the decisions.'

Or words to that effect. I didn't end the experiment just because the neighbours complained. I didn't give in when colleagues complained that my kids were uncontrollable after a lesson with me. After all, it would take time for the youngsters to come to terms with a new way of working. I finally stopped when I realised that amidst the noise and mayhem no-one was learning anything — and almost everyone in the class was perfectly content with that situation.

So, back to square one. And then, gradually, through different jobs, different parts of the country, my teaching style developed. What I have tried to put into effect, in the mature period of my career, is my belief about the needs of the children of the underclass. It is the antithesis of the concept of the facilitator teacher. It is the dominating teacher.

Successful teachers of the underclass impose themselves on their classrooms. There are a variety of ways to do this, according to the teacher's personality. Small people, with quiet voices, do it. Large people, with megawatt volume, do it another way. Some do it by means of organisation, some do it by means of charisma. They are all determined to be the centre of attention. They all impose the understanding that their wishes are paramount, that when they speak, pupils listen, that when they instruct, pupils obey.

Of course, like every other description in this book, that is a generalisation. Even the dominators need to apply the three Cs with the most troubled and difficult. But everyone in these classes realises that such allowances are justifiable exceptions to the rules.

'Teacher of the underclass required — only the extraordinary should apply.' Without entering the eternal debate, 'Teachers — born or made?', let us agree that such people need all the qualities of successful teachers anywhere, but to a greater degree. They must be fitter, more resilient, more charismatic, better organised, more committed, than teachers elsewhere. They must be prepared to impose themselves on the pupils.

Let us be frank — only a few can do all this, can be all this. Naturally, to have such qualities is not sufficient for successful classrooms. The teacher needs appropriate lesson content as well. It is pointless gaining the attention of the class unless it is then asked to do suitable things. Leadership qualities may not be sufficient, but they are certainly necessary.

The point is to exercise control. Control, of course, is an unpopular word within contemporary British society. The simple sociological truth that social control is a basic need of any society is very unfashionable. This has led to a lack of analysis of the social control function of a variety of institutions, including education.

In a school community of motivated and willing learners, control is not the central issue. This does not mean that social control is not operating, merely that its locus is elsewhere than the school. In general, socialisation within the family has produced a commitment to conformity which includes sharing the aims and values of the school. Educationists have neglected to analyse the implications for schools whose pupils are from cultures where such controls have not operated.

There is a problem here with respect to the culture of teaching. Inner city schools are staffed very largely by teachers with a social commitment. They have a vocation to help the underprivileged. In some schools, and not only Church schools, there is an almost explicit definition of the teacher as missionary. There is a strong tendency for that vocation to move through sympathy for the pupil to excusing the pupil, superimposed on the very real dilemma of what might be appropriate aims for the education of the underclass.

The result is often a rejection of a concept of control in favour of an emotional commitment to a democratic pedagogy. Incidentally, this confused thinking is nowhere more obvious than amongst some of my colleagues who are active on the far left. They are often committed to giving pupils 'freedom', sometimes to the point of anarchy. To step inside their theory for a moment, are they unaware of Marx's contemptuous dismissal of the lumpenproletariat as a reliable revolutionary force? Do they not consider that a revolution could only be made by a highly disciplined force? Surely, what they want is not mindless vandals, but highly focused saboteurs. A *laisser-faire* school culture will not produce the latter.

What schools in such areas must face is the reality that, even if they do not aim to produce a revolutionary army, their aims can only be met by forcing their pupils to take on new values, and to develop a commitment to educational success. Such a process requires *control.* Lots of it.

A democratic style of pedagogy is linked to the concept of teacher as facilitator. The concept is inculcated in young teachers through training and, more importantly, socialisation into the culture. It is widespread in the city, particularly in primary schools, but it is by no means universal.

For one thing, it is self-destructive, for it amplifies the stress I have described. However, there is a more important cause for the spread of democratic pedagogy. It is simply this. Many teachers do not have the qualities to use a dominating pedagogy in front of pupils from the underclass. Many teachers find that they just cannot stand in front of a class and gain its attention. The class just will not listen.

Who will admit this? Few.

The truth is, I suspect, that the kinds of individual and group work which are organised by the teacher as facilitator can be operated in a classroom where whole class teaching cannot be achieved. Many secondary schools in London still use the SMILE (Secondary Maths Individualised Learning) scheme developed many years ago. Some maths teachers still believe in it, others continue to use it because it's the only resource there is in their school. It consists of a vast bank of worksheets, carefully organised, and accompanying monitoring stationery. It is a living project, continuously updated. Pupils are supposed to find their worksheet from the filing cabinet, complete it, mark it, correct it where necessary, and move on to the next in a sequence. They work at their own pace, and completely individually. The teacher's role is to ensure the materials are in place, to support individual pupils, and to monitor their progress.

The rationale for SMILE is that it enables each pupil to progress, making sure one concept is understood before moving to the next. The reason for SMILE, initially at least, was completely different. ILEA developed SMILE to cope with an endemic shortage of qualified maths teachers. (Plus ça change…) It permitted pupils to self-teach while being supervised by teachers who could learn the organisation of the scheme, even if they could not transmit mathematical concepts themselves. It also permitted apparently purposeful endeavour while obviating the need for class teaching.

I give the example of SMILE, not because it is unique, but because it is one I have used myself. In other secondary subjects, teaching styles have developed which cut out the time consuming, exhausting and ultimately unsuccessful task of gaining and holding the attention of the whole class. Worksheets which convey the instructions for the lesson are a commonplace.

Recently, the debate about didactic teaching — whole class teaching — has come to the fore, driven by politicians. The government is no doubt aware that a previous attempt to address the issue sank virtually without trace. The 'Three Wise Men' report, published in 1992, was a measured discussion of primary practice. It had many ideas which merited discussion and development. At the level of schools, it stimulated neither.

No doubt pressure on schools to change will become more real. No doubt the liberal culture of teaching will be a target. Now, whole class teaching is just what the minister ordered, and this prescription produces an uneasy feeling amongst teachers.

It is not so much that most of them do not believe in class teaching: it is more that they may have swallowed the state telling them what to teach, but they will not accept the state telling them how to teach. The organisation of a classroom is a matter of professional judgement, judgement developed by years of training and experience. It is not a simple issue; most teachers will adopt an organisation suitable for a particular task, and use a variety of approaches according to the type of lesson, so that small group or whole class is almost a meaningless question. Teachers do not believe that the government — any government — can say with entitlement or with understanding that one is better than the other.

However, it is not just any old whole class teaching which seems to be the new holy grail, but interactive whole class teaching. Avoiding the cheap quip that it is impossible to conceive of a room containing 31 people in which there is no social interaction, there are some significant problems about this. It implies that there should be a uniformity of experience for a class.

This is the exact opposite of the orthodoxy which has been thrown at teachers for some time, of the need for a differentiated experience. Using the Ofsted whip, inspectors and advisors have demanded that lesson plans show 'differentiation' — how the lesson is to contain the variations necessary to meet the variety of needs and levels of attainment of all the pupils in the class.

Early on in this assault, some tried to claim that lessons were satisfactory if they contained 'differentiation by outcome' — in other words, the pupils' responses varied according to their attainment. This, however, was rejected as a cop-out, so that teachers have strained every imaginative muscle to produce materials suited to the various needs. Differentiation demands attention to the individual pupil. It is the basis for much recent development, such as the Individual Education Plan for pupils who are placed on a school's register of Special Educational Needs.

No doubt the supporters of interactive whole class teaching would argue that it is all a question of balance, that some whole class work should be followed up with differentiated individual or group work. Such a response at least starts to address the fact that the question is a complex one, and it enables teachers to reassert their rights to determine pedagogy. It is indeed a question of balance, but if teachers are expected to spend most of their time in front of the class while it attends to one activity, they cannot simultaneously be expected to produce differentiation. If the DfEE/Ofsted machinery of persuasion and enforcement exerts serious pressure on this issue, it can expect resistance.

Part of the reason, no doubt, will be the resentment that the same machinery has for some years been exerting the pressure on differentiation, and another U-turn would be unwelcome. Another part, however, is the simple practicalities. Whole class teaching demands a level of compliance and order in the classroom which, as we have seen, is partly or completely absent from many schools in the inner city, at least. This fact cannot be discussed with those who impose orthodoxy, but is an important determinant of how teachers work.

There is no learning without order. There can be no whole class teaching without order.

Smaller classes

Apart from teaching style, but linked closely with it, is another factor which is essential at classroom level, if unpopular with the government. In the school for the underclass, classes of more than fifteen pupils begin to be unmanageable.

I do not pluck this figure out of the air, or merely jump on some smaller class bandwagon. I do not suggest that this size is necessary in all this country's classrooms, or even all those in the city. It is just my professional judgement that schools for the underclass need that class size if they are to stand a chance of breaking through.

Why? Every class in such schools has a large proportion of pupils whose behaviour as individuals reflects their cultural position. By that, I mean they behave as angry, stressed, oppositional people. They are all indifferent to or opposed to schooling, just as they are to the other major institutions of society.

Their anger and opposition may be expressed in a variety of ways, as we have seen. For some, it is open and direct; the teacher is challenged, disobeyed, defied. For others, it is indirect; the child seems abnormal, with bizarre, inconsequential behaviour, apparently oblivious to the teacher. It is possible for the superteacher to dominate even such young people — but not when they are in large groups.

Every teacher knows what I mean, even if there is no research which addresses precisely this issue. With a compliant group of pupils, classes in the thirties are manageable, using whole class teaching, from a control and output point of view. The problem with such groups is the time needed for monitoring, assessment, and recording. With a few difficult pupils, the manageable number is reduced. And in my experience, in the school for the underclass, the manageable number is fifteen.

This amounts to a proposal to double the number of teaching staff in such schools. Before the gasps over the cost implications, let me go further.

More teachers

Every teacher in these schools needs a considerable amount of the working day without class teaching responsibilities. One reason is the difficulties of performing in such classes; they produce exceptionally high stress levels, which make the teachers ill. High absence and high turnover are features of these schools, which militate against the stability and consistency which are such vital elements for success. All teaching is performing, but what actors are expected to perform live, for five hours daily? Performance should not be expected for so long in these schools.

There are more important direct reasons in terms of pupil attainment. Teachers often do not want to hold up the flow of a lesson to react to minor infractions of the rules by individuals.

'See me after the lesson/at lunchtime/after school'. Then the teacher takes time to explore why the pupil was late for the lesson/did not hand in homework/has dropped in standards lately/was behaving inappropriately/seems upset and so on.

On occasion, the structure of a lesson may allow this to take place at the time. With a class with low levels of deviance, the teacher can find time outside the lessons. One feature of the school for the underclass is that staff are overwhelmed by the amount of this kind of deviance. There is simply not the time to chase it, particularly if pupils are not inclined to comply with requests to meet the teacher outside the lesson times. There are just too many pupils who arrive late for the lesson for them to be followed up. There are too many more serious incidents, like a fight or assault, to be dealt with.

Owing to a set of peculiar circumstances, I once worked in such a school where I had responsibility for only two classes, which I taught for three hours a week each. I was also in a position to use other time to support this teaching. I was relentless.

I established my routine, and used many hours in following up every single deviation from it. I abolished lateness by offering bags of praise for the punctual, and by keeping late pupils behind, or, if I had to release them for another lesson, by finding them at the end of the session and keeping them at that time.

Always. Without exception.

I was able to mark homework on the day it was due in, and I had the time to find those who had not handed it in, discover the reason, and take action. I also had the time to implement the agreed action, for example to send home a letter in the case of repeated failure.

Always. Without exception.

It was not the severity of the sanction which affected behaviour, it was the certainty of it.

I applied similar techniques to each area of class routine. I even managed to attack internal truancy, to the extent that the few most recalcitrant pupils started to absent themselves for the whole day rather than just bunk one lesson. (Was this success?)

I like to think that, in two terms, I turned those classes round. I established a high degree of order in the classroom. The quantity of output increased markedly, and I could devote much more attention to the pupils' attainments, which improved. The point of this story is not to demand recognition as superteacher. The point is that achieving compliance is possible, but requires at least as much time as is occupied by the lessons.

The reason teachers in failing schools are overwhelmed is that one lesson generates many incidents and issues which should be followed up, but that lesson is instead followed by another, and another, and another, and the day ends, and the pupils disappear, and the teacher is exhausted, and there is a meeting, and the next day's lessons must be prepared and the paperwork completed. Work for these teachers is indeed a combination of the treadmill and the stocks.

But forget about teachers' welfare for a moment. What is required, if the children of the underclass are going to be harried into achievement, is for their teachers to be freed for about half the school day to undertake the harrying. So if we take together the proposals for class size and class contact time, I am suggesting an approximate four-fold increase in the number of teaching staff in these schools.

I suppose this is where the decision makers react, 'He would say that, wouldn't he' and close the book. However, the problem of working class underachievement has been with us always, and any attempts to solve it have been largely ineffective. For some time now, governments have been using a rhetoric of attacking the issue, in the shape of a general drive to raise standards. If the government wishes to continue at the level of rhetoric, it can try more dynamic sounding ideas in the area of inspection of and support for schools. If, however, it really wants to make a difference, it has to start from the realities and look for real solutions.

Those solutions must start in classrooms. They must include the content and method of teaching, with implications for training, but they must also include the question of the staffing levels needed to bring about substantial change. I do not make these proposals because I believe it is necessary to spend to solve every problem. I make them because they arise from my experience of the situation.

More supervisors

As described earlier, a striking feature of failing schools is the kind of activity in the school's public spaces, the corridors, halls, staircases, and outside the buildings. Boisterous behaviour in the playground outside session times is one thing — and schools need to be ever alert to the quiet bullying and worse which is not advertised in the same way. It is the number of pupils in the public spaces during lessons which is noticeable.

One problem about this is that there is likely to be a larger proportion of pupils in this type of school who have reasons for being out of class which would be regarded as legitimate by teachers. Pupils of the underclass are less healthy, more likely to need the school nurse. Pupils of the underclass are more likely to be upset because of domestic trauma — a parent has left, or suffered violence, or there has been a dramatic incident in the home or the neighbourhood. I do not wish to be dismissive of the agonies of those involved in highly publicised tragedies at schools, but 'Small disaster, not many dead' is a frequent occurrence at many inner city schools. Pupils genuinely seeking support in such circumstances may nevertheless wander the school for some time before finding the adult supporter.

Then there are the borderline teacher-sanctioned movements. Shortly after a lesson starts, the pupil announces she has left her coat/bag/book/pen with a friend/in another room, and requires to retrieve it. Particularly when the item is necessary for the lesson, does the teacher, in pursuance of the three Cs, permit the pupil to leave? As described, there may be a period of ten minutes at the start of a lesson when large numbers of pupils are making their way across the school, imperceptibly at times, from their previous lesson.

However, those hanging around during lessons are mainly just simple internal truants. They have registered at the start of the day. They have attended a lesson they fancied. They have voted to miss a lesson they don't fancy, but have nowhere off-site they want to go.

None of this is new. I recall, twenty-five years ago, when a neighbouring school slipped into trouble. Part of the authority's reaction was to trawl its schools for eight of the toughest and most experienced senior staff it could find, and to second them to the troubled school for a term. A major part of their role was to patrol continuously, in pairs, the school's public spaces, returning pupils to classrooms.

Since then, I have found no better answer to this problem. Unfortunately, this is another expensive measure. In theory in many schools, senior staff undertake this task on a rota. In practice, in the failing school, senior staff are submerged in serious incidents and difficult problems which prevent them from carrying out the routine.

In reality, effective patrolling of public spaces can only be undertaken by additional staff. The question arises, is it necessary to employ expensive skilled teachers for the job? Perhaps not. It is necessary, however, to employ staff who carry sufficient authority.

Experience teaches us that midday supervisors who carry out that function during the lunch break have a difficult time. Perhaps they need proper training, which is rare, for they do not find it easy to gain compliance, and they frequently need to call on support from senior teaching staff. It is certainly important for patrolling staff to know the pupils by name as far as possible, and to have gained some legitimacy with them. On the whole, it is the superteachers who have been in the school some time who achieve this position.

An alternative is to take the route of using the kind of supervisors who could best be described as security guards. In some schools in the United States, these guards are armed, but there might be an intermediate between that and the untrained ladies who are often midday supervisors in this country. I think it would take a lot to make guards acceptable, but there is plenty of evidence that conditions in some of our schools approach those where it would make sense.

Although I do not address it in this book, the general problem of security from intruders with malevolent intent is growing. What does require review is whether some of the tasks allocated to teachers in English schools, including some supervision, are an efficient use of a very expensive resource. The truth is, they are allocated such tasks because the budget does not stretch to employing others to do them, but we must analyse just how much of the work now done by teachers could be done just as well, and more cheaply, by others.

The crucial point I make about staffing the school for the underclass is this: those recalcitrant pupils must be overwhelmed by the sheer weight of numbers of adults around the building. They need a high degree of confidence that, wherever they wander, they will be noticed by a member of staff and guided onto the path of righteousness. They need to see that, while they are in a classroom, a member of staff will be giving each of them attention, and being impatient of lack of attention to task. They need to know that, out of the lessons, their will be members of staff who can meet their emotional, psychological, and other needs.

I understand that this sounds hopelessly unrealistic. Yes, of course. How could society ever afford to provide the schools for its most needy with that kind of staffing level? Why, the only places where that happens are the schools for those young members of our society who, on the whole, are born with every conceivable advantage, and before taking one step inside any school are bound for wealth, privilege, and ease: the public schools, of course. I am not the only person who finds this odd.

Recruiting the teachers

There are two financial reasons why my proposals are unrealistic. The first, and obvious one, is the reluctance of the government to restore the funding of education to the levels it once enjoyed. The decision to increase spending by £19 billion over previous plans still leaves education spending at a much lower proportion of Gross Domestic Product than in 1980. There is also some doubt as to how much of that welcome increase will filter through to schools to spend on their 'core business', as opposed to being allocated by the government for other pet schemes.

The second reason is that the current allocation system, the local management of schools scheme, is simply too inflexible an instrument to allow the necessary funding of underclass schools. Of course, factors are built into the funding formula which allow them to receive more money than other schools, but the degree of differential is totally inadequate.

On the other hand, no progress is possible in these schools until they are able to recruit a larger staff and retain a stable workforce. Commentators on the national teacher recruitment crisis now commonly suggest that a substantial increase in pay is needed for good teachers who wish to remain in the classroom, and of course this would help in the underclass school too. My belief is that some additional pay incentive on top of this necessary national rise might help in recruiting staff to the underclass school, but I have shown that the real problem is retention.

Against the problems faced by the staff, their pay packets are relatively unimportant. The classroom stress, the workload connected to individual pupils and institutional needs, can only be ameliorated by smaller classes and more non-contact time. Teachers would stay, however difficult the pupils, if the task was to manage less than fifteen pupils, and they were free for half the school week to recover, and to chase up pupils as necessary.

As in all schools, underclass schools would find it easier to retain their staff if they had better working conditions. They need quiet working areas with good access to equipment such as phones and computers. They need better facilities for rest and recovery, with proper refreshments. Teachers in underclass schools constantly say that they are not valued. This is partly an issue of management skills, but partly an issue of the environment they suffer. Now that David Puttnam has taken up this cause, perhaps there will be some progress here.

The staff need to feel valued in other ways. They need sensitive management, even more than in other schools. They need their real training needs to be given a high priority.

None of these ideas for retention are new. They are simply good practice for any employing organisation. Good practice is very largely lacking in our schools, and creates particular difficulties in our underclass schools. When staff there are given a reasonable workload, and feel that they are valued and the enormity of their task is recognised, they will stay.

At the same time, such measures would contribute to a considerable decrease in both long-term and short-term absence. This would greatly enhance staffing stability, and in itself make a significant contribution to pupil performance.

Leadership

So the school for the underclass needs a very substantial increase in staffing if it is to make the kind of difference required of it. As we know, however, in the English structure, the headteacher is a crucial determinant of the school's success. If the school for the underclass needs superteachers, it undoubtedly needs super-headteachers. Unfortunately, it seldom gets them. I shall not repeat the accumulated wisdom on the ways in which the headteacher contributes to the school, but there are two points which have not always been clearly understood.

In the eighties, long before it was fashionable, the ILEA identified thirty schools which gave cause for concern. In twenty-seven of them, the core of the problem was weak or absent leadership. It is no accident that schools identified by Ofsted as failing almost always have a change of head after, or sometimes just before, the inspection. The fact is that leading a school for the urban working class is a very difficult job, and only outstanding people can manage it.

Another fact is that the education world has still not developed effective ways of selecting people for headship. Until recently, the interview was still the universal method — hence too many heads' offices occupied by superficially smooth talkers without the substance. Now there is the tendency for candidates to be set a variety of tasks, such as in-tray exercises. The problem is that the crucial aspects of the head's role, managing staff and leading pupils, are rarely adequately tested.

Too many headteachers simply do not have the interpersonal skills to deal well with these tasks. Now we have the National Professional Qualification for Headship. It remains to be seen whether it resolves this issue, or whether once again those who are good only on paper will gain advancement to the cost of all in the schools they lead.

It is even more difficult to attract the right candidate to take over the failing school. In too many cases, the incoming headteacher is not the right person to lead a school for the underclass. When that happens, the school is in an even worse situation than before it was judged to be failing. The employer must show loyalty to the head it has picked, and it will be some time before it becomes sufficiently obvious that a further change is necessary.

The second point is closely related. It is the question of the qualities needed in a headteacher of a school for the underclass. Local authorities and governing bodies have largely accepted the apparent implications of the local management of schools, which make the headteacher in effect responsible for the budget and the employment of staff, as well as the leadership of a team of teachers. They now look for people with management skills.

Whether this is the way forward for schools in general is one question; whether it is the appropriate approach for the school for the underclass is another question. There is no doubt that there is a difference between leadership and management, and I am certain that in teaching, the former is more important than the latter. The emphasis on management skills for headship now constitutes a serious handicap to the improvement of performance.

It is partly a matter of what tasks headteachers are expected to perform. I cannot be the only person who considers it self-evidently ludicrous that a professional, highly trained, experienced and skilled person in teaching young people, in organising the work of other teachers, in questions of what ought to be taught and how, should be expected to be an expert in building maintenance, contract compliance, employment law, accountancy and financial services, and many other issues far removed from classrooms.

The nonsensical dogma of local management has had a number of ill effects on schools, but one of them has been to make the role of headteacher virtually impossible, and the job increasingly unattractive and hard to fill. Under local management, headteachers are subject to no effective controls, and while this autonomy was naturally attractive when the system was introduced, many heads now realise that freedom from 'the office' is an illusory benefit.

The problem is also about the style of headteachers. Heads as managers are to be found in their offices moving paper. Managers from industry and commerce are said to be good models, and various schemes for work shadowing and job swapping are supposed to provide good experience for managers of schools. We even have the notion, now applied in the independent sector, that the head of a school does not need experience or knowledge of teaching, because managing a school is just like managing any other organisation.

There is a very common misunderstanding within schools that management is the same thing as administration, because the latter is what senior staff spend a lot of time doing. Why skilled professionals paid £30,000 to £40,000 a year should spend hours compiling statistical returns and routine forms is a question never answered.

What schools need is a bit less management and a bit more leadership. Ability to teach is not a quality required in headteachers these days, but ought to be vital. A headteacher who can handle a difficult class not only attracts the respect of staff and pupils alike, but will have the skills to deal with difficult individual pupils. As I shall show, this is vital in the school for the underclass. The ability to support and inspire the staff is not the same thing as the ability to implement the competence, sickness, and disciplinary procedures when necessary.

It is interesting that the same themes are emerging in other public services which seem to some to be over-managed. The recently retired HMI of Constabulary, Sir Geoffrey Dear, has written, 'Management is about logistics, scheduling and costings, but leadership is about winning hearts and minds and instilling a sense of common purpose... We have too many managers and not enough leaders.' I am fairly sure that that if we had an HMCI of Schools of stature and independence, the same things would be said of schools.

Just as their classrooms need dominating teachers, so schools for the under-class, in my view, need dominating headteachers. They need people who are very visible, command immediate attention from teacher and pupil alike, who can impose themselves on pupils. In short, the major item on the person spec-ification is charisma. Heads who do not have the budget management skills could employ someone who does. But if the head does not have charisma, then the pupils will know that the buck stops with someone who doesn't have what it takes, and the authority of every member of staff is diminished.

This is not an iron law. I once worked in a school where, one day in May, I was teaching a class from Year 8. The head popped in the room for a quick chat, which was unusual for any teacher, and particularly unusual for me. I was gratified that the class carried on with its task without undue disorder. When he had gone, one lad said, 'Eh, sir, who was that fella?' It transpired that after almost two years in the school, the class had never seen the head-teacher.

However, this did not prevent the school running extremely well. This was a huge school, in terms of roll and geography, and was run on a real house system, with pupils taught in house groups and focusing on a house base. Pupils related to their Head of House, who performed the role of leader. And, boy, were they charismatic! Some of them terrified the new staff, let alone the pupils. The headteacher had a clearly defined role which largely excluded dealing with children. It worked then, but could not work now, because schools are not large enough and there is insufficient in staff budgets to permit such a staffing structure.

Secondary schools have a system of discipline with escalating sanctions and referral. Class teachers are supposed to keep their own order for routine matters, but pass to more senior staff more serious matters. Good discipline systems will specify this more precisely. There is a chain of referral, which typically will be class teacher — head of year — deputy head — headteacher. In most schools one reason for referral onwards will be the refusal or failure of a pupil to comply with a sanction.

A feature of the school for the underclass is the very large amount of time occupied in dealing with this behaviour. Perhaps the original offence was minor — being late for a lesson, say. Let us suppose the teacher concerned was not so weighed down with other things that the matter was ignored or forgotten. The pupil was instructed to stay in for a short time after school. The pupil did not appear. The pupil was found the next day, made some lame excuse, and was told that failure to appear on the next occasion would result in referral to the head of year. The pupil failed to appear. The teacher used the appropriate document to inform the head of year of the circumstances. The head of year then sent for the pupil, who failed to appear, thus requiring more time to be spent in locating him. The head of year then instructed the pupil to attend a year detention, but the pupil failed to turn up... So it goes on.

Let me make the point again. In many schools, this sort of thing may happen occasionally. It is a nuisance, and takes the valuable time of senior staff, but it can be dealt with. In the school for the underclass, at any one time there are many, many pupils involved in this scenario. It is the weight of numbers which makes it impossible to deal satisfactorily with every case. In such schools, the problem is compounded by the likelihood that senior staff will also be dealing simultaneously with more than one serious incident, such as a serious assault on other pupils or staff, bullying or extortion, shoplifting or robbery committed by pupils during the school day, and so on.

But back to our referral chain. Finally, perhaps, the deputy head will pass the case to the head. A minor infringement has resulted in a major case of defiance of the authority of the school. In fact, the original offence was itself an expression of rejection of that authority, but in many cases the operation of the three Cs prevents escalation.

Now no-one pretends that this is an easy situation to deal with, but the head's actions at this point determine many things about the future of that pupil, the staff who have dealt with him, and the whole school's disciplinary system. It doesn't matter whether the school spends its budget effectively. It doesn't matter whether very efficient sounding management structures are in place. It doesn't matter whether the head has an MBA. The only thing that matters for the future of the school is whether word goes round the playground and the staffroom that the pupil has been dealt with effectively.

That will be achieved only if the head has the personal presence, when confronting the pupil or parents, to make things happen. If the head is successful, then all the way down the chain to the class teacher, the next confrontation over lateness for lessons is just that bit more likely to be resolved successfully. Any other pupil is just that bit less likely to be late for a lesson. The staff will have just that bit more time to ensure that pupils are on task. The long, slow, step by step process of improving attainment will be under way.

If, on the other hand, the head is unsuccessful, the reverse process occurs. In my experience, a major cause of class teachers giving up on dealing with the minor problems is the knowledge that they will receive no effective back-up when incidents go up the line. When they do give up, we have a failing school, where order is maintained only in pockets occupied by the superteachers.

It is an empirical fact that schools for the underclass are frequently headed by people who do not have the necessary presence. The fact is that many of these schools maintain their identity over many years, through whole generations of staffing. Perhaps we should conclude that the job is simply beyond any normal professional. It is certainly the case that many of the headteachers brought in after the school has failed Ofsted do not have the qualities I have described.

All of this casts light on the government's ideas about reviving failing schools, as well as local authority policy. They both recognise the importance of leadership, but do not seem to have come to terms with the two vital issues I have discussed: what kind of leadership, and how are the right leaders appointed?

Recruiting the headteachers

The problem of attracting headteachers to the school for the underclass is perennial. Currently, the problem has become a crisis. Schools advertise two or three times without finding a suitable shortlist; hence the development of headhunters. It would be a mistake to fall into the trap of concentrating on the material benefits of the job. After all, teachers are not in it for the money. The current tendency to offer 'attractive financial packages' is an attempt to overcome all the other disincentives for potential applicants, but if the job itself was more attractive, financial incentives would be unnecessary.

Offering large sums of money brings its own problems. Under the rules of local management, the local authority cannot fund such an appointment, but the school, particularly if it is an Ofsted failure, is likely to be in financial difficulty. Paying 'over the top' in such circumstances is likely to create further budget problems, as well as resentment from the rest of the staff, since the school will have gone through a redundancy trauma.

No, the way to attract people of the right calibre to inner city headships is to eliminate the disincentives. The obvious one is the negative attitude of the government, aided and abetted by the press. While we are thinking about effective management, it does seem strange that the government does not seem to know the principle of accentuating the positive and avoiding public criticism of staff. However, this topic is done to death, and I do not intend to repeat the widespread condemnation of the name and shame tactics; just to add that teachers have found it particularly depressing that the new government, which came into office with such a mass of goodwill, has not learnt how to make the most of it. We want to see the doing, not the sloganising, particularly when the slogans suggest that part of the programme is to identify those elements who would 'obstruct progress' and to liquidate them. The fact is that fear of public condemnation is a very strong reason for avoiding appointment to a school which is or could be in special measures.

There are particular aspects of this for schools in the inner city, related to the league table mentality. Since these schools are always going to be at the bottom of any league table, they will continue to attract negative attention until the market ideology is replaced by a community ideology which will make league tables unnecessary.

However, I am not certain that the answer is the opposite tendency, public acclamation of the successful headteacher. Almost by definition, the successful head will engender the notion that the school's success is due to the staff as a whole. The award of a honour, be it a knighthood or something more humble, by the monarch may well be regarded with some embarrassment as undue personalising of a team effort. A more useful and appreciated response would be positive reporting of the school as a whole by local media, as co-ordinated by the local authority.

A stronger disincentive, I believe, is the content of the job itself. It is true that many headteachers and their professional associations are somewhat confused about this issue. On the one hand they complain about the workload attached to the job, which according to the government takes more than 60 hours a week on average. Often, the problem is as much in the kinds of work required as in the hours, which brings us to the other hand: headteachers still widely support the local management of schools which has brought most of the extra work and unwelcome kinds of work.

Headteachers collectively have to make up their minds. If they want to remain autonomous bosses of small businesses, they must expect the kind of workload that goes with it. If they want a return to the more limited role of responsibility for the educational aspects of the enterprise, they have to demand changes to the current devolved structure. In my view, the job would become much more attractive if it were to be more limited in scope, with others responsible for buildings, employment issues, and so on.

Current local management rules place further difficulties in the way of making the job of inner city headship more attractive. They prevent local authorities from using their headteachers in imaginative ways for the good of the local service as a whole. Since governing bodies are responsible for hiring and firing, the authority has no power to deploy heads to best effect. Let me give an example.

Appointment to the headship of an inner city school could be a life sentence. However effective the head is, the league tables will not show it, and the reputation of the school will be a drag on subsequent movement to another post. At the same time, early retirement has been made much more unlikely.

Potential applicants might feel that after, say, seven years they will have given everything they have to offer, and will be exhausted mentally and physically, but that there will be no escape route at that time. If only the local authority was the employer! It could offer, formally or informally, permanent employment with a seven-year assignment to the school. At the end of that period, the head and the authority could discuss a further period in post, or redeployment to another, less stressful headship, or another post in the service using the head's particular skills and experience. Such an arrangement might well appeal to potential headship applicants who are prepared to make the enormous commitment necessary, but are not prepared for a life sentence.

There are other possibilities: an authority could offer a sabbatical after a certain length of service, but it is unlikely that a locally managed school could afford such an offer. The virtual impossibility of redeployment under local management causes difficulties and costs in a number of ways, but the inflexibility is a major block to sensible staffing of the school for the underclass, and to headship recruitment in particular.

In the end, the only answer to the question of how to encourage able people into inner city headship is the simple one. It is necessary to make the job more attractive. Teachers are not the kind of people who are particularly motivated by material rewards, which is why gimmicks will make only marginal differences. The job has to be made less stressful, less demanding of time, and more rewarding in the psychological sense. Incidentally, the same applies to teaching in general.

As there are very few people with the qualities and skills which enable them to be successful headteachers of difficult schools, demand far outstrips supply, and a large proportion of those in post at any one time are not up to it, including many who either have been or would be perfectly adequate in less demanding schools. It might be concluded that there is something basically wrong with a situation in which a job is so difficult that it is beyond all but a few.

It might also be concluded that there is something basically wrong with the dominant ideology surrounding turning round failing schools. The message is that failing schools have incompetent teachers and an incompetent head. Replace the head, let the new incumbent replace the staff where necessary, and problem solved. My message is that the staff would be perfectly competent, within the definitions of this story, in many schools across the country. Only superteachers and superheads make out in the school for the underclass.

So the issue of headship is even more central for schools for the underclass than for schools in general. We need to have new person specifications, or rather much more old-fashioned ones, and we need to find new ways of attracting and selecting them. And when we have done that, we would be foolish to imagine we had solved the problem of such schools.

The improvement package

Let me summarise my list of essential prerequisites for improving the failing school. Many of them centre round their staffing needs. The current situation is untenable.

We need to attract the best teachers; not defined as those who know most about their subject, nor as those who have lots of qualifications in education; these schools need teachers with personal magnetism and determination, whose firm fairness will appeal to pupils, whose charisma will overcome pupil resistance. In particular, we need to attract headteachers with the same qualities, to a higher level. We need selection techniques which do pick out those who can manage, in the sense of handling people, so that they can support their staffs and win the respect of their pupils.

When we have attracted the necessary staff, they need carrots, not sticks. They need really useful training, in classroom management, interpersonal skills, dealing with aggression, and so on, and in teaching basic skills of literacy. They need really useful monitoring and advice, so that inspectors, having observed their work, can make specific and positive suggestions for improving their practice. They need a sensible workload, so that they have time to follow up their lessons, and time to recover from the stress of teaching. They need a reduction in unnecessary work. They need a better working environment.

Their schools need a radical increase in the number of staff, to give them a more even chance of imposing their collective will on unwilling youngsters. They need the ability to implement a more suitable curriculum, so that pupils are learning knowledge and skills which are of use to them. They need support in implementing a more suitable pedagogy, one which demands participation and progress from all pupils.

And their teachers need recognition. Along with some other professionals, these are the people who confront poverty, alienation, conflict and opposition within society. These are the people dealing with the darker side from which others turn away. They have nothing to show for it, as far as the bourgeois world of league tables is concerned. They deserve the public thanks of politicians, who create the dark side of society as well as the bright, and of the nation as a whole.

A marginal gain

It is not defeatism, but realism, to remember after all this, that even in schools which have come closest to the models I describe, there has been only limited success. I have seen outstanding leaders, magnificent and highly talented staffs, schools much better resourced than most (though never to the degree I advocate). I have seen schools in which most teachers gave of themselves to pupils, before school, after school, weekends and holidays. In these schools, I have seen young people from the most terrible backgrounds lit up by the comprehension that there is another kind of life out there, in that other society, which is within their reach.

Sometimes.

We must be realistic. Those successes are the exception that proves the rule. We must be honest. In the underclass school, the large majority of pupils leave school as initiates of the underclass culture. They are alienated. They are hopeless. They have rejected school, the teachers, and all they stand for.

I believe that my list of improvement methods would make a difference. A little difference. A few more pupils could be separated off from their peers and convinced that there is another way. I salute those people now coming into the profession who are prepared to work so hard, content that the little difference they will make is worth the sacrifice.

I have passed through that stage. I look for more.

Within the current parameters of political debate, these may be the only methods which are both possible and positive in their impact. They are not enough. They cannot achieve the government's aims of a radical improvement in educational achievement, and an attack on social exclusion. We must look a little more widely for ideas about improving the education and life chances of the underclass.

8

THE ANSWER BEYOND THE SCHOOL

I HAVE TRIED TO SHOW IN THIS BOOK that the situation in many inner city schools is desperate. I have also tried to show that this is only because the situation in the communities which they serve is desperate. Many of the commonly proposed and attempted solutions are doomed to failure. The inspection regime only exacerbates the problem, and local management militates against appropriately targeted action. The levels of human resources needed to make a difference in these schools is far beyond any apparently possible input.

I do not want to be thought a pessimist. I have written this book because policy has to be based in realism, and I believe the real picture has not been painted in the past. If my painting is considered a useful likeness, some possible ways forward suggest themselves. Part of the scene is an explanation of the persistence of the situation, or something very like it, since the start of compulsory education more than a century ago.

In the previous chapter, I looked at some of the measures which could be taken within underclass schools to produce some improvement, however marginal. Now I turn to a vital component in the administration of our secondary school system which helps to create the underclass school. Then, I return to the most important reality for the inner city: educational attainment is closely determined by aspects of the cultures of the classes at the bottom of our social hierarchy. It can be affected principally by economic and social policies which alter the life chances of these classes, and therefore attitudes to education.

The failure of parental choice

We have tried parental choice, and it has failed. We need a better way to plan school admissions. Parental choice was the cornerstone of the Conservative desire to create a market in education. By forcing on schools formula funding largely dependent on pupil numbers, schools would become responsive to parental wishes. Since parents would act as rational economic beings in consuming education, they would select, given sufficient information about the market, the product with the best exam results. This would force up attainment in all schools.

It would be silly to deny that this form of market has affected schools, although this is not the place for a full analysis of all the effects. From the point of view of the hierarchy of schools within the city, the effect has been to sharpen and deepen the divisions, and to speed up the rate of change within it.

Oversubscribed schools have tended to become more oversubscribed. This is not always the blessing that might be imagined. For example, consider a school which has a socially mixed intake, within a local authority where admissions are decided principally by distance from home to school. As the school becomes more oversubscribed, the radius of the distance from home circle is reduced, in some cases to half a mile. The school, in effect, is bound to accept pupils only from the immediate vicinity of the school. This reduces the chances of an socially mixed intake, and undermines the comprehensive virtues which made the school popular in the first place. Of course, schools situated in favourable locations might welcome the more middle class intake with the further improved league table position, and even greater popularity, although it might seem difficult to understand any advantage to a school in being oversubscribed by 300% as opposed to 50%.

On the other hand, undersubscribed schools have become more undersubscribed more quickly. The major problems then become a budget shortfall, which may require messy and demoralising staff reductions, as well as severely limiting a school's options, and an influx of pupils expelled from or not wanted by other schools, further worsening the pupil mix. Both of these add to the downward spiral. As noted previously, it is far easier to circle down this hierarchy than to climb up.

Even from the point of view of those who believe in 'choice', the present system needs reform. The proportion of parents satisfied with their child's secondary school allocation is steadily falling, and the number of appeals steadily rising. I believe that this reform is one vital element in moving towards a schools system in the cities which can raise attainment for those underachieving the most. I have no intention of making specific proposals about admissions procedures for secondary schools. I believe that a debate is required, involving the various interested partners. Parents, who increasingly realise they were sold a pup in the previous reform, form one group. Education authorities, who have to try to make the monstrosity work, and pick up the pieces when it doesn't, form another.

For schools everywhere, the major aim of the reform must be to reduce the present free-for-all in secondary transfer procedures. This cannot be achieved until the breakaway individualists in grant maintained schools and the like are returned to the administrative fold, but the ability of local authorities to make rational procedures which suit almost everyone must be enhanced.

For the schools which are the focus of this book, more radical solutions are necessary. Policymakers must become aware of the histories of such schools, and note their persistence through all kinds of administrative change. That alone should curb any tendency to proclaim that another change marks the end of the sink school.

It is difficult to see any system which retains a nod towards parental choice completely eliminating class biases in individual schools, but we need a much stronger impetus towards a social mix in secondary schools. Many people would see the history of bussing in the United States as a warning against going too far down the road of enforced social mixing, but a change in the present balance between directed social mix and parental choice is essential.

It will be important not to listen to ideologues who use slogans such as 'freedom' or 'choice' to prevent rational debate on secondary admissions policies. We have moved about as far as possible towards choice for parents at 11+, and they are discovering the choice is illusory. A school can accept a finite number of pupils. If more than that apply, then some form of selection operates. This selection is then by the school, not by the parents. Thus the growth of parental cheating by using a false address, or inflated property prices in the catchment areas of oversubscribed schools, although these are phenomena of the suburbs rather than the inner city.

Such a change will only become possible with the overthrow of the present tendency to perceive schools as independent of each other, indeed as competitors. The secondary schools in each area need to be seen again as a single service, very expensively funded by the state, which together must maximise life chances for all the country's young people. Admissions policies must not be framed only for that small minority of parents which has the ability and the will to bend systems to its advantage.

Incidentally, my view is that some parents do not think clearly when seeking the 'good' school for their offspring. This is why London teachers had contempt for the decisions by the Blairs and the Dromeys (Mrs. Dromey née Harman) regarding their children. In terms of the hierarchy of schools, the Oratory and St. Olave's are as close to the top as it is possible to be without being public schools. Indeed, within the ILEA, the Oratory was always regarded as independent in practice. In so doing, they betray great ignorance of the realities of educational life in state schools. This is scarcely surprising,

I suppose, if their own backgrounds, and those of their social circles, are from outside the non-selective state system.

Let us exclude from this discussion the small number of failing schools. Taking almost any other local comprehensive school, if middle class parents were able to study the examination performance there of children like their own, they would find the results as good, for all practical purposes, as in the 'top' schools. By that, I mean that their children would achieve sufficient high grade GCSEs, and then A levels, to qualify them for entry to their chosen university. It is simply the fact that schools which produce few undergraduates have had few pupils of undergraduate potential. If more pupils with that ability enrolled, the school would produce more academic success. It really is as simple as that. The Blairs, the Dromeys and their like may well feel that they wish for other things from their children's schools, but they are simply wrong to imply that attendance at a local comprehensive school would damage their children's life-chances.

I do not wish to make inflated claims about the value of comprehensive education in terms of social integration. Some crude versions of this in the past have rested on absurd notions of social class. Nevertheless, it is undeniable that there is some social benefit in socially mixed schooling. Young people have a better knowledge and understanding of the varieties of class (and ethnic) communities within our society when educated together. Without wanting to extend discussion of this, I think it is generally accepted that this limited outcome is a good thing for society as a whole.

This argument on choosing schools is not based on an assumption that parents should have no rights over their children's' education. I assume the contrary. The point is that parental interest should be focused within the school, rather than between schools. In other words, parents need to understand that the best way to ensure the optimum educational outcomes for children is not to try to select the best school, and then leave it to get on with it. The best way is to realise that all schools have their strengths and weaknesses, and to show an interest in the child's progress and to intervene where necessary. I know that this will be unpopular with many teachers; after all, 'interfering' parents can be a huge nuisance. Yet I think all teachers realise that if their practice is sound it should not be a huge task to explain it to the satisfaction of parents.

A new look at admissions

The notion of a current imbalance between parental choice and the needs of all children is not new. In the early nineties, papers for the National Commission on Education (by Walford, and Adler) made the same point.

There are a number of ways that admissions could be organised which recognise both factors.

Perhaps using the criterion of best placement to meet the child's needs might be at the centre of such arrangements, as long as the needs are not just interpreted by the parent, but by teachers, the child, and the receiving school as well. This process is already in place for children who are the subject of a Statement of Special Educational Need, although I should emphasise that no-one would argue for a system of admissions to be similarly tortuous. In such an arrangement, entry to oversubscribed schools would be on the basis of the degree of need.

Those who think such a procedure would be hopelessly time-consuming are clearly unaware of the time and effort, not to mention money, spent by secondary schools at the moment in their efforts to attract pupils. Whatever the stated educational aim, primary-secondary liaison, which involves a lot of work for a lot of teachers, is all about recruitment. Programmes of visits for potential parents and pupils, advertising in the local press, glossy brochures, all use up valuable resources.

The admissions procedure ought, as at present, to be set by the local authority, but within a much more explicit framework of its aims for all its children. This might involve agreement with schools about their specialisations, on the understanding the local authority would have some powers to ensure a balance across a given area. It should involve some form of mechanism for ensuring an appropriate social mix. It should also involve the power to resource schools differentially, depending on their specialisation and intake; LMS formula funding is too blunt an instrument for this.

If a new admissions system largely abolished enrolment by competition, it would be easier for schools to be frank with parents about their problems as well as their achievements. This is necessary if parents are to be engaged as allies in the struggle to improve attainment. Many parents would be aghast if they saw what really happens in classrooms and corridors, and their disapproval is essential if change is to occur.

To conclude, then, it is necessary to build a new system of admissions which takes account of parental choice. At the same time, it must not raise such a right above all other needs, not should it accept motives for choice which are illogical or socially unacceptable. One outcome of such a reform must be an attack on the longstanding phenomenon of the socially homogenous school for the underclass.

To put it positively, those pupils who reject state education need to be in a school community where they have the opportunity of learning its value. Let me repeat the reasoning behind my insistence that reform of admissions is a basic requirement for transforming the failing inner city school. As long as such schools are populated exclusively by children from the underclass, there is no possibility that the institution can overturn the anti-learning culture they bring to school. As I have shown, at the moment such schools are simply overwhelmed by a variety of forms of resistance. Teachers have an impossible task because they have no allies in presenting society's dominant view of the value of education.

An alternative is to implement my proposal in Chapter 7 to quadruple the number of teaching staff and provide extra supervisory staff in such schools. However optimistic we might be about the government's economic growth dividend, it is difficult to imagine that kind of investment being politically possible. Without investment of that order, the staff will never be able to gain and maintain the ascendancy. The only way to make the struggle more even is to reduce the volume of oppositional forces within the school.

I do not underestimate the difficulty in producing a system that will break down generations of definition of these schools as sink schools. It is more difficult for a school to move up the hierarchy than down, but if we can find an administrative way of producing the mixed intake first, then the upward spiral can be stimulated.

There are two separate effects of a better social mix. The first is that there will simply be fewer pupils in the school who will present problems requiring more attention than is available. There will be fewer pupils minded to truant. There will be fewer pupils minded to be on the corridors during lessons. There will be fewer pupils in classrooms who refuse to co-operate. There will be fewer pupils who are inclined to aggression or violence. If the reduction is sufficient, the staff will be able manage disorder and create an atmosphere of order.

The second is that working class pupils will ally themselves (in terms of how they actually behave) with the staff version of the purpose of schooling. In short, they will provide an alternative role model to that of dissident. They will provide an additional demand for order in the classroom. They can create with the teacher a new version of the role of the pupil, by conforming with teacher demands for learning. They will produce exam success. Their subsequent careers in further and higher education or employment will provide illustrations of an alternative future to the street and social exclusion.

All of this is problematic. There are many difficulties at every stage of the process I suggest. However, those who protest that the difficulty amounts to impossibility are obliged to make some alternative suggestion. The situation I describe cannot be allowed to continue: the government's requirements for higher standards for all cannot be met unless this problem is addressed. The Ofsted regime provides no answers, and nor will the new stress on pedagogy.

Exclusion and alienation

Reforming admissions would help to get round the problems of educating the underclass. It would not solve them. If that is our aim, we must first remember the persistence of patterns of failure within state education.

Advanced societies are very highly socially differentiated, most importantly by social class, which describes relative access to economic power and wealth. Education systems in such societies perform the essential task of reproducing this differentiation in each generation by means of qualifications, thus enabling the distribution of individuals to various levels of occupation. It follows that it is essential, it is inevitable, for schools in total to produce pupils with a range of qualifications or, to put it another way, *to produce both successes and failures*.

We know that compulsory education provides every individual with an opportunity to get to the top, regardless of social background. We also know that the lower the starting point, the more difficult, and the more infrequent, the climb becomes. It is possible to analyse the history of state education in this country as a process of easing the access to that journey, although the process remains far from complete.

We must never forget, however, that whatever the opportunities for *individuals*, advancement for *all* is absolutely impossible. Schools will always have the task of allocating young people to their place in society, and there is limited room at each place. This includes placing the least qualified in the lowest stratum of society, which now is the urban underclass.

Many teachers, especially from secondary schools which are at the sharp end of the process, have recognised this hard truth. No amount of high aspiration about fulfilling the potential inside every child, or about education being 'leading out', can hide the fact that the state spends billions of pounds on schools *largely in order to achieve this sorting*, and to prepare children for their place in society.

Some would argue more strongly, that social control is indeed the first task of schools in a capitalist society. In this view, the school in the city acts to repress the working class, to attack working class values, and to control resistance to the state and its agencies, while preparing working class young people to accept their subordinate and exploited position within society.

It is not necessary to hold that view in order to describe the situation in our failing schools in terms of the reproduction of class cultures. The underclass is now an excluded class. Objectively, the chances of significant upward mobility for an underclass child are very small, and becoming smaller. It is not irrational for members of the underclass to perceive state education as irrelevant to their lives, and to oppose schools. It is not irrational for underclass young people to resist conformity to a middle class institution which does not reach their real and awful concerns.

The antipathy between the underclass and their schools is produced at least as much by rejection and resistance on the part of the community, as by any attempts at control or repression on the part of the schools. Rejection and resistance are the responses of an alienated minority to many manifestations of the state and the lives of the comfortable majority. Ever since the introduction of state education the lowest stratum in society has understood that schools are about failure and maintaining its low position.

It must be emphasised that reform of the curriculum or the assessment system, for example by means of giving parity of esteem between academic and vocational qualifications (as if such parity could be accorded by bureaucratic decision, rather than by popular assent), or any other changes in schools, can do nothing to alter significantly this situation. The education system's inevitable task is to sort people, and in our society that must mean to sort into social classes. It is almost inconceivable that those sorted into the bottom group should not resent this.

The grim conclusion is that *we shall have failing cities, and failing schools within them, as long as we have our present economic and class structures.* As I said previously, the immense efforts which have always been made by the staffs of failing schools can have all-important results for a few individuals, and marginal positive effects for their pupils as a whole. These effects are insignificant when compared with the size of the problem and the possible impact of social and economic policies which deal with the underclass as a whole.

Education cannot compensate for society

Circumstances have worsened considerably over the past twenty years. The profoundly misconceived reforms of the government have created multiple difficulties with very little compensating gain. More important, as far as the education of the underclass is concerned, economic and social policy has widened class division and deepened class conflict in a reverse of all the trends of the previous century. It is not necessary to advocate revolution as the means of solving the problem of the underclass: what is necessary is to produce full employment and a major reduction in economic inequality.

The greatest boost possible to education in the inner city would be an attack on inner city poverty and alienation. The social phenomena I described in Chapter 2 are obvious to all. The economic trends behind them have been encouraged by government in a wholly short-sighted policy whose rhetoric is repeated by the new government, but which must be overturned to prevent increasing social dislocation. The collapse of unskilled work, or to put it another way the substantial reduction in employment in Britain, is not the direct result of government, but results from the inexorable development of global capitalist competition. It affects all advanced post-industrial societies. The solution offered at the onset of this process was a combination of retraining and state welfare support, but both are failures.

The period of mass unemployment has coincided with a substantial growth in educational qualifications. More pupils than ever achieve success at 16+; more than ever go on to success at 18+; and no fewer than a third of Britain's young people now gain a degree. The result is simply qualification inflation. GCSEs do nothing but determine the entry level to the next stage of education. A degree, which so recently was a certain passport to secure and comparatively lucrative employment, now guarantees nothing. Meanwhile, employers complain that they cannot find staff with suitable skills. Quite apart from anything else, this suggests a crisis within further and higher education.

It is simply not true any more that a reasonable set of results at school gives young people a good start to their economic lives. They know this. For those in the middle and working classes, the necessity of going further is understood and, more or less grudgingly, accepted. But for those from the underclass, for whom the acceptance of the value of education at all is a struggle, the realisation that leaving school is just the start is just one obstacle too far.

There is still unskilled work. It is now of a different kind from that available twenty or thirty years ago. Instead of general labouring, we have the fast food outlet, and telesales. It is at least as insecure as in the past, and the general level of wages is comparatively lower, forced down by the state of the employment market and the import of techniques such as zero hours contracts to ratchet up the exploitation and uncertainty.

In the past, unskilled work was available for a family's major earner. Now, this marginal work is done by those formerly marginal to the family economy. Part-time jobs for young people are the standard kind of unskilled work. Even here, we see the exclusion of the underclass, as students earn the money to enable them to fulfil the role of young consumer to which they aspire. So families of the underclass have an ever lower chance of any kind of employment.

The simple truth is that there are too few jobs to go round. No amount of rhetoric about skills revolutions and raising standards will alter that fact. There are more people who want a job than there are jobs. Education never created a job: it is employers who create jobs, and increasingly they organise their businesses with fewer and fewer jobs.

Welfare failure

The complementary answer, state welfare, is now seen for the failure it is. The state has been unable to maintain welfare payments or entitlements at reasonable levels, simply because the numbers demanding them are unsustainable. The repeated redefinition of entitlement to unemployment benefit is often noted as a means of fiddling unemployment statistics. For the poor themselves, the loss of the benefit itself is somehow more important. After years of struggle, the government has now succeeded in making it respectable to debate the impossibility of continued state welfare in its present form.

It is not so much the absolute level of benefits which is the problem. As clever kids writing for right-wing publications sometimes show by example, by getting through the maze and jumping all the fences, it is possible to receive sufficient benefits to allow the well-organised middle class fit young man to eat healthily for a week. Incidentally, I think we ought to take as an indictment of our education system the degree of ignorance of basic sociology illustrated by this kind of attitude to the poor, which is often associated with the 'they're only in that condition because they're stupid or lazy' concept.

It is the accumulation of material circumstances which generates the way of life of any social group, including the poor. Their problem is not that for any given week, the money they have only stretches by dint of high levels of organisation and good luck. Their problem is the continuation of that week after week, and year after year, in their household, and all the other households in the district.

Any group's way of life is a rational response to the circumstances it finds itself in — and if there is some stability in the circumstances, there is a stable response which becomes a culture. Progress will be made in attacking poverty when the behaviour of the poor is accepted as a reasonable response to their situation.

No, the absolute level of benefits is not the most important factor. It is their value relative both to average earnings, and to the earnings of the wealthy. In contrast to past eras, the wealthy are somewhat visible to the poor. In many cities, pockets of housing for the rich are found close to the slums. The poor are more mobile, and are more likely to notice the rich. The mass media also present frequent images of wealth, although often giving the implication that extreme wealth is something for a tiny few, mainly showbiz stars, while the stars of business seem to hide away.

The fact is that the disparities between the rich and the poor have increased under recent governments to a degree unknown in modern times. The boom of the eighties allowed a massive increase in the number of British millionaires. It did not go unnoticed amongst the poor, not least because since then benefits and wages for unskilled work have been forced down.

Average earnings in Britain also continue to grow, both absolutely and relative to the cost of living. Those who are in work have more spending power each year. Let us ignore the hiccup caused by feelings of insecurity, arising from the perceptions of the vast majority of employees both in both public and private sectors that their jobs are not safe, certainly in the long run. Greater spending power is welcome news to the wealthy, who are relying on the continuing ability and propensity of the people to consume.

Pressures to consume continue to grow, in all kinds of subtle as well as more obvious ways. Dominant culture in the western world is now saturated with the values of consumerism, and the British people play their part. We have heard one or two voices suggesting that the level of consumption relative to the level of saving is not a good thing for the economy in the longer run, but there is no hint of serious political action in this direction.

Extreme wealth, and average wealth with spending sickness, thus confronts the poor at all times. The poor also have access to the mass media which are clearly important organs for consumption persuasion. More than ever, then, the underclass is in the position of having no spending power but receiving constant exhortations to spend. It is, to use that ancient but ever useful concept, relative deprivation which both reinforces the exclusion of the poor from society and also catalyses their anger at their plight.

Worklessness and culture

The combination of relative deprivation and long-term unemployment helps to create contemporary underclass culture. Recently, journalists have increasingly used as a measurement of deprivation in such communities the percentage of families whose offspring have no memory of a family member in work. Permanent unemployment creates a different culture from uncertain, casual and occasional employment, which until recently was regarded as the position of society's lowest stratum. Permanent unemployment justifies the term social exclusion, for it denies to the underclass even that largely illusory ambition to belong, which may have bound people to their society in some small way in the past. Permanent unemployment forces the underclass to seek permanent alternative solutions to their economic needs, or where solutions seem impossible, to seek disassociation from this cruel world.

The result is a culture which is destructive and self-destructive. It is a culture of antagonism, of aggression. Some forms of behaviour arising from this culture were described in Chapter 2. They are known to all, they are clearly observable and, for the delight of millions and to sell a paper, are broadcast to those who miss them personally. What is missing from the broadcast, however, is any social analysis of the behaviour, any link with the social and economic structure which produces it. Thus the media acts like a horror comic: here's the story, isn't it awful, it's so gruesome, JUST LOOK! — and keep looking when we come to the adverts. Vice in a vacuum. Others may point at the moral vacuum, but my concern is the social vacuum.

Are drug taking to excess, rape by children and street robbery just individual pathologies? I think that, from the 'string 'em-up' bloke in the pub to the earnest discussion of the decline of morality at the dinner party, there is some back-of-the-mind understanding that greater forces are at play. Unfortunately, the media provide no sociological context for those people to use.

The government is no better. Government responses to those shocking elements of underclass behaviour are based on an individual pathology model. Policy on drug-taking concentrates on how to deal with the individual drug-taker, coupled with the most crass campaigns which aim to say, 'Don't take drugs, because they're bad for you.' Do those who dream up this kind of campaign really imagine that those who live in drug communities do not know their effects? Of course not. They have to give the illusion of action, while avoiding the real questions about the origins of the will to seek release from reality. It is possible to analyse policy in a variety of areas, mostly connected with law and order, and see the same processes at work. As long as the government uses models of deviance based on the individual, these policies will fail.

The response of government to failure is to redouble efforts. The problem is that given the inability of the forces of persuasion in our society to exercise sufficient control to alter behaviour, control increasingly has to be by more naked power, or, as home secretaries like to say, the full force of the law. The political froth has it that prison overcrowding is the fault of the previous government's detailed policies on sentencing. We shall see: as time goes on, our present prison accommodation will be insufficient to deal with violent offenders alone. The police will come under increasing pressure, as their work of crowd control comes more to the fore. As more and more youth excludes itself in hopelessness from mainstream education and mainstream society, mini-riots become an everyday part of life. Law and order will require ever more control mechanisms which will affect everyone, and further separate the alienated from the included: identity cards, road blocks, curfews, labour camps, an escalation of police weaponry.

Does anyone really believe that the problems of disorder and social breakdown in our society, largely connected with the urban underclass, can be solved by such action? The government will not admit it, but everyone knows it: we have to look beyond the superficial symptoms. The government will not admit it, because to do so would involve basic questions about the economic and social structures of our society.

At this point, of course, my marxist friends start jumping up and down. There is no alternative, they say, these inherent contradictions will lead to a politicisation of the exploited classes and the overthrow of the regime and the capitalist system it supports. There are members of the rank and file of the fringe marxist groups who continue to believe that this is possible. Well, maybe...

But while we await this transformation, could the government do something to confront the realities? Not unless it openly accepts the fact that the problems of the urban underclass, including its alienation from the education system, are the result of its exclusion from the global capitalist economy of which the rest of society is a part. It might be possible to find a strategy for inclusion which does not involve employment, but this seems unlikely.

The only alternative is to persuade capitalist enterprise to change tack. The iron imperative for capitalism to force down costs continuously is destroying modern society, for all classes except the ruling class. What is the use of cheaper goods, most of which we do not need but are persuaded to want, if we cannot enjoy their use in peace and security? Material goods must be for the benefit of their users, but it is an inescapable feature of human society that their manufacture must also be for the satisfaction of the producer. Capitalism has reached the stage where it excludes an ever greater proportion of the population from work, but pressurises those in work to intolerable levels.

Can the British government do anything about this, even if it wishes? If not, could the European government, or the G7 governments? Exactly what are the power relationships between these and the global corporations? Such questions are beyond the scope of this book. My point is that there is no solution to the problem of the failing school in the failing city without attention to the global economy.

Adherents of the government point to the one nation rhetoric of the prime minister. A minimum wage would help, surely? There are two problems with the minimum wage. The first is the level at which it is set. By definition, if the minimum wage is to help the low paid it must be set at a level which will be strongly opposed by employers. The second is that the minimum wage does nothing to help those never in receipt of a wage, and as we have seen this is a condition increasingly affecting the underclass. This is not to say that a minimum wage is of no use; rather, that it is of marginal use, and does not impinge upon the issues raised in this book.

The other policy which is of direct interest is the job creation programme. In the past fifteen years we have had plenty of these. The function of job creation schemes has been to create the image of activity on unemployment and a another chance to reduce unemployment statistics.

At least the New Deal accepts the necessity for job creation by employers, which is the only way of addressing the issue. On the other hand, the proposals for lifelong learning avoid the crucial issue of forcing employers to accept their responsibility to provide the training that is needed for their employees, which is an integral part of modern work. The pace of technological change makes it quite unrealistic to expect education and training institutions to produce job applicants with the appropriate skills. It is possible, but unlikely, that some EU legislation can make a little difference of that kind.

I started with Alison and Victoria being uncouth and negative in a French lesson. I end with questions of global political economy. As a teacher, I can do nothing about the world economy, although by working myself into the ground I have managed to reduce the negative behaviour of some Alisons and Victorias.

Whether or not the government can affect the development of world capitalism, it can do some things. I am convinced that some members of the government, and many members of the governing party, know of the things I have described. I believe that they share my anger, or at least remember their own anger, at the misery of those at the bottom of our society. Like me, they have cried at the waste when seeing teenagers with lives already empty or ruined, young people already layered with a hateful hardness. For twenty years, they have waited for an opportunity to take action on inequality and exclusion. I demand that they now take that action.

This book was born in anger and tears and frustration. As a teacher, as a veteran of inner city schools, as a survivor of a failing school, I have stood accused of failure. Remote powers have described me and my colleagues as ineffective, as the problem, as letting down the country and its young people.

This book is my way of standing up and saying, yes with pride, that I do not accept your propaganda. We have struggled on behalf of those young people struck down not by us, but by society and its hierarchies. By sticking it out, we have proved our commitment to them, while society has walked by on the other side. The schools we work in have been ineffective not because of our inadequacies, but because they are not the site of the problem.

We can be proud, because sometimes our struggles do make the crucial difference for some of our pupils. The victories look small to outsiders: an ex-pupil holding together a job and a marriage; an ex-pupil who has stayed out of prison; an ex-pupil who has been successful in further education. For them, and for us as teachers, these are massive achievements.

But we must say more. We must shout, and shout until the powerful listen, that we have been unable to save the many from the scrap heap. In truth, they were born on an ugly and unnecessary scrap heap, and they will remain on it. Our wealthy society could sweep away the scrap heap, the ugliness, and the failure, but requires the will of the controllers of capital to do so.

Perhaps that is asking too much. If so, I demand just one thing. I demand that those who give their all in the failing schools of our failing cities be recognised. I demand that our heroes be honoured. And given respite.

Index